THE GUIDED SKETCHBOOK THAT TEACHES YOU HOW TO DRAW!

ROBIN LANDA

The guided sketchbook that teaches you how to DRAW!

Robin Landa

Peachpit Press

Find us on the Web at:
www.peachpit.com

To report errors, please send a note to:
errata@peachpit.com

Peachpit Press is a division of Pearson Education.

Acquisitions Editor: Nikki Echler McDonald
Production Editor: Becky Winter
Development Editor: Cathy Lane
Proofer: Emily K. Wolman
Indexer: James Minkin
Design Manager: Charlene Charles-Will
Composition: Danielle Foster
Interior Design: Dawnmarie McDermid
Cover Design: Denise Anderson, DesignDMA
Cover Illustration: MItzie Testani and Robin Landa
Interior Illustrations: Denyse Mitterhofer and Robin Landa

ISBN 13: 978-0-321-94050-6
ISBN 10: 0-321-94050-4

9 8 7 6 5 4 3 2 1

Printed and bound in the United States of America

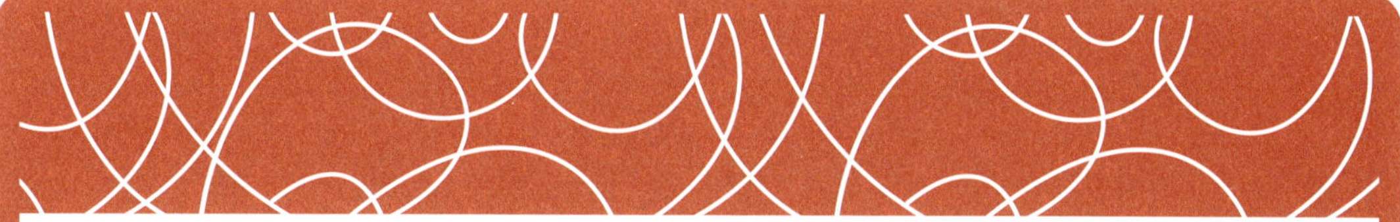

Dedication

For my darling daughter, Hayley, and you, dear Reader. I hope you fall in love with drawing.

Acknowledgements

I am grateful to the following distinguished people who contributed to this book and your drawing experience:

Polly Apfelbaum
April Allen
Roberto Bertoia
Liz Blazer
Robert Brinkerhoff
Janna Brower
Stefan G. Bucher
Michael Cho
Lester Cohen
Lyman Dally
Jim Dawkins
Allan Drummond
Jonathan KYLE Farmer
Rose Gonnella
Glenn Griffin
James Gulliver Hancock
Jessica Helfand
Alexander Isley
Kristina Junkroft
Nancy Lampert
Lorin Latarro
Greg Leshé
Laura Letinsky
Ruth Lingford
Kendra Meyer
Denyse Mitterhofer
Barbara Nessim
Josh Owen
Hsinping Pan
Shell Redfern
Diamond Rivera
Ted Rose
Mark Romanoski
James Romberger
Henry Sene Yee
Mary Ann Smith
Roberta Smith
Jennifer Sterling
Jessica Stockholder
Yoom Thawilvejakul
Frank Viva
Ellen Yi-Luen Do

I extend an extra thanks to the visual artists who contributed marvelous drawings to this book: Liz Blazer, Stefan G. Bucher, Lyman Dally, Jonathan KYLE Farmer, Rose Gonnella, Greg Leshé, Denyse Mitterhofer, Hsinping Pan, Diamond Rivera, Mark Romanoski, Mary Ann Smith, Jennifer Sterling, and Yoom Thawilvejakul.

Nikki McDonald is the kind of editor every author hopes for—thoughtful, super-smart, and helpful. I am grateful to her for believing in this project. My thanks to the good folks at Peachpit Press: Cathy Lane, Charlene Charles Will, Becky Winter, and Danielle Foster.

Great thanks to my stellar design, illustration, and production team: Denise Anderson, Dawnmarie McDermid, Laura Menza, Denyse Mitterhofer, and Mitzie Testani.

For their support of this project at Kean University, I respectfully thank Dr. Dawood Farahi, President; Dr. Jeffrey Toney, Provost; Dr. George Arasimowicz, Dean of the College of Visual and Performing Arts; Prof. Rose Gonnella, Executive Director of the Robert Busch School of Design; Dr. Susan Gannon and the Office of Research and Sponsored Programs; my colleagues; and the wonderful Kean University Robert Busch School of Design alumni and students.

For their help and support, I thank Ryan Daniel Beck, Steven Brower, Paul Doto, Samantha Gniazdowski, Stephanie Knopp, Martin Holloway, Carlos Alberto Hernandez Malagon, Jayme Kilsby, Margrethe Lauber, Melissa LoCasio, Jason Ortenberg, Robynne Raye, Deborah Rivera, Karen Sonet Rosenthal, Ria Venturina, and the Clifton Benevento Gallery. Loving thanks to Denise Anderson, Paula Bosco, and my husband, Harry Gruenspan.

But most of all, I am indebted to my beloved daughter and thoughtful reader, Hayley, who carefully edited my manuscript and created wonderful drawings based on it.

"Drawing may be the most intimate and honest of all art mediums. Its lightweight materials enable artists to work almost anywhere and often give their efforts a truth-telling transparency that exposes the very nerve endings of their talents. Sometimes drawings function almost as a kind of signature, distilling an artist's sensibility to its essence. Sometimes they express gifts visible in no other medium."

—*Roberta Smith, Co-Chief Art Critic,* The New York Times

Table of Contents

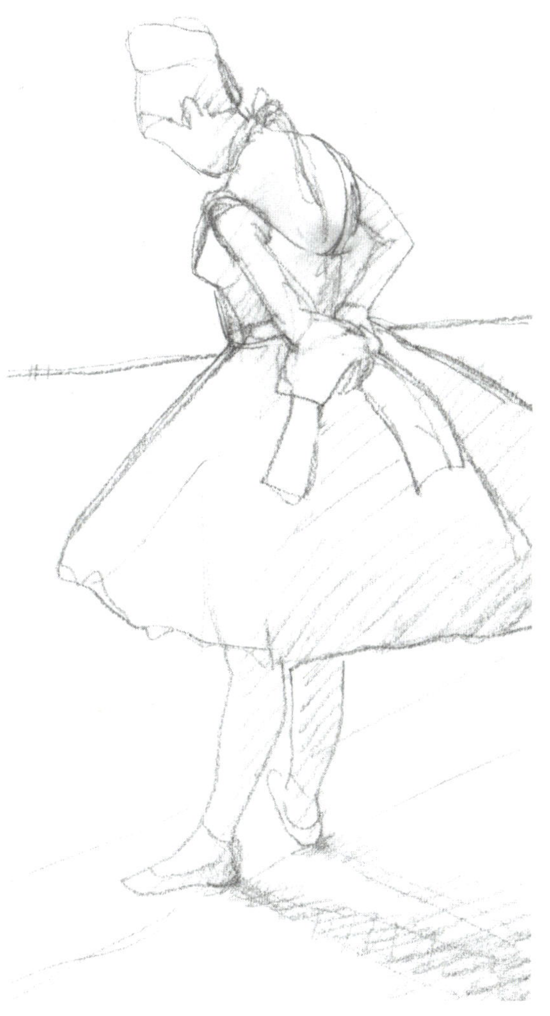

Essential Materials and Tools

It's time to gear up. You'll need most of the following tools to do the exercises in this book.

Analog Tools

Paper

It's OK to draw in this book. I want you to! But to practice you should have additional drawing paper. Most drawing paper will do for beginners, such as a drawing pad of (acid-free) paper that takes pen and ink, pencil, crayon, charcoal, light ink washes, and markers. A handy size for most subjects (and laps) is 11x14- or 14x17-inches.

Or go with graph paper for use with pencil or marker, which provides a modular grid for visual measurement.

A couple of the prompts in this book call for heavier paper or art board, such as bristol board, which is a lightweight board with two working surfaces, front and back. Other prompts call for tan or gray toned paper, which you can purchase ready-made or make yourself. Using a big brush, you can hand-tone paper with cold black coffee, cold tea, or thinned ink or water-based paint.

Drawing board

You can place your sketchbook on a table or on your lap when drawing, but you may prefer to use a drawing board. Inexpensive Masonite sketchpad boards afford a sturdy sketching surface. But such a board is optional.

Pencils

Pencils are available in varieties that range from very soft (8B) to extra hard (6H). Soft graphite pencils make darker marks and are great for quick sketching. Harder pencils retain a sharp point and make lighter lines; they're good for detail work and straight lines.

Get these: 6B; 2B; B; H or F; and 2H. (When I don't specify which pencil to use, try several to learn what each can do and which you prefer.)

Pencil sharpener

A hand-held, all-metal sharpener for standard size pencils (8 mm) works well for sharpening artist's pencils.

Cylindrical charcoal sticks

Vine and willow charcoal sticks are good drawing tools for rapid visualization and creating broad areas of tone, and they are easily removed with a kneaded eraser. Some artists prefer compressed charcoal for its strength. Charcoal is inexpensive so you can experiment with different kinds. But you'll need to spray them with a nontoxic fixative for permanence (see next page).

Black and White Conté crayon

Conté crayons are made from a blend of natural pigments, kaolin clay, and graphite, and are used for rapid sketching as well as shading on a variety of paper surfaces. These crayons are popular drawing implements. You can sharpen the crayon's tip to a chisel point (using a sandblock) for detailed work, or use its blunt tip or its broad side.

Erasers

White plastic eraser

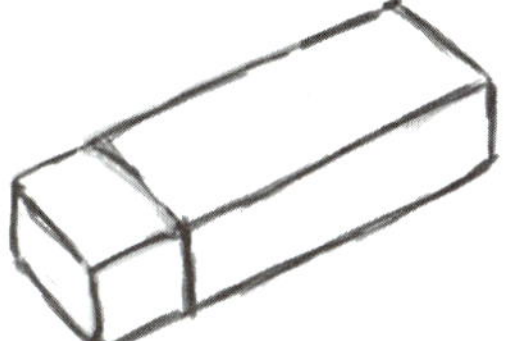

These erasers remove graphite marks cleanly and completely from paper, and they are my recommendation for working with pencil.

Kneaded rubber eraser

These knead into any shape, erase marks fairly cleanly, and pick up residue. They self-clean when kneaded and are excellent for use with pencil, vine, and willow charcoal.

Pink Pearl eraser

Soft and pliable, this eraser removes graphite marks and has beveled ends for better control.

Gum eraser

This is an all-purpose eraser, but it leaves a good deal of residue.

Markers

Many visual artists favor fine-point black markers (nontoxic) as sketching or drawing tools. Experiment with different brands; some have less drag than others. Markers are *not* easily erased. Consider their marks permanent.

Wide-nib black markers (nontoxic) are good for experimenting and drawing boldly as well as for fill-in work.

Nontoxic markers are available in packs of assorted colors in both fine-point tip and wide-nib. An inexpensive small assortment is fine for working in this book. Or you may prefer student-grade colored pencils.

Nontoxic workable fixative

This variety of fixative is workable (you can continue drawing on top of it after applying it) and nontoxic; SpectraFix Natural Casein Spray Fixative brand is one example. Fixative protects your work. Even if you use a nontoxic fixative, be sure to use it in a well-ventilated room or outside.

Black India ink

Black India ink is highly pigmented, opaque permanent ink that can be diluted with water and used with most brushes. It's good for wash drawings and drawing experiments. For wet drawing media, I recommend it over black acrylic paint.

Black and white acrylic paint and acrylic medium

Acrylic paints are water-based, fast drying, and diluted with water or acrylic medium, which lengthens drying time and increases flow. (For the exercises in this book, acrylic medium is optional; you can dilute acrylic paint with water or use India ink instead.)

Brushes

It's good to have a round, pointed brush as well as a flat brush. Sizes of brush vary by manufacturer. (Avoid small brushes, which encourage drawing from your wrist rather than your arm.) Artist-grade brushes can be costly; student-grade brushes are fine for learning. (If you have old, battered brushes, those can be used, too, and are excellent for experimentation.)

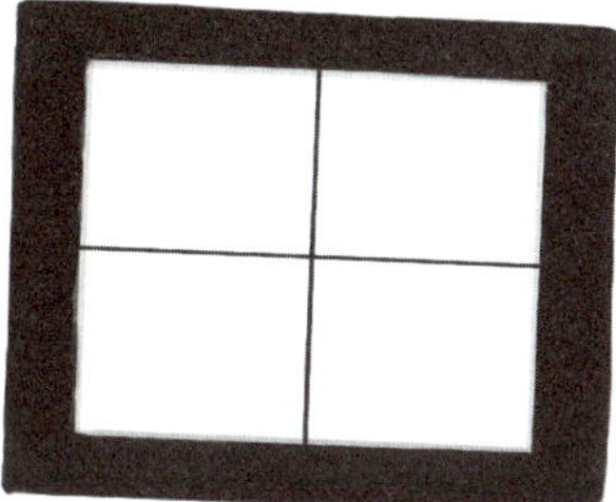

Drawing aids (optional)

Viewfinder

A viewfinder is an artist's tool—a clear, lightweight plastic grid window for visualizing compositions in thirds or other modular unit grids. It allows you to isolate a section of a scene, or separate a scene or space into modules, which helps you determine where elements fall on the page. You can make a viewfinder with clear, hard plastic and a dry erase marker or purchase a readymade one. One brand is the QuicKomp Artist's Drawing Tool, whose side also can be used as a straightedge.

Rule of Thirds grid

The Rule of Thirds is an asymmetrical compositional plastic grid that you can use as a viewfinder to aid the positioning of a focal point in the composition. You'll learn more about it in Chapter 1. You can purchase this or make one by ruling the grid onto clear, hard plastic.

Four-quadrant grid

A four-quadrant modular grid viewfinder, made of plastic or heavy acetate, allows you divide what you see into manageable, smaller parts. You can purchase this or make one by ruling the grid onto clear, hard plastic.

Wooden artist's model

This is a wooden, fully jointed and proportioned figure (available in various sizes), that you can pose to help you visualize form.

Digital Media

Digital pens and tablets

Some digital pens and tablets emulate the feeling of drawing on paper. Purchase the largest tablet you can afford. Some people are comfortable drawing with a mouse or trackpad, but digital pens and tablets offer better drawing experiences than either of these options.

Always check software needs and specifications before purchase of this equipment.

Pen-on-screen

Some digital pens allow you to draw directly on the surface of a high-performance LCD display.

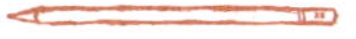

Elizabeth Blazer

{ANIMATOR, DESIGNER, HTTP://WWW.LIZBLAZER.COM/}

"Draw yourself doing the impossible."

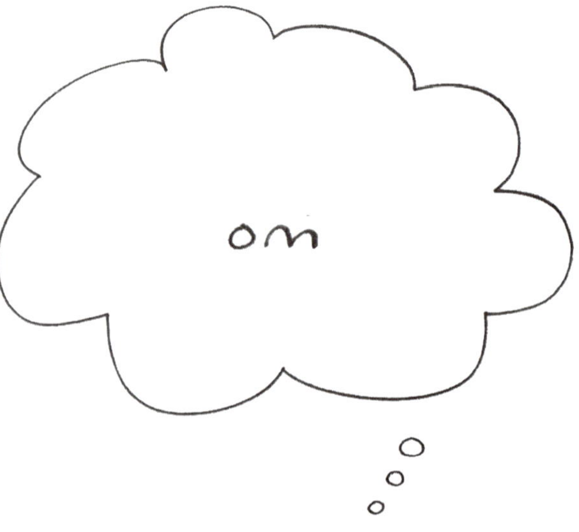

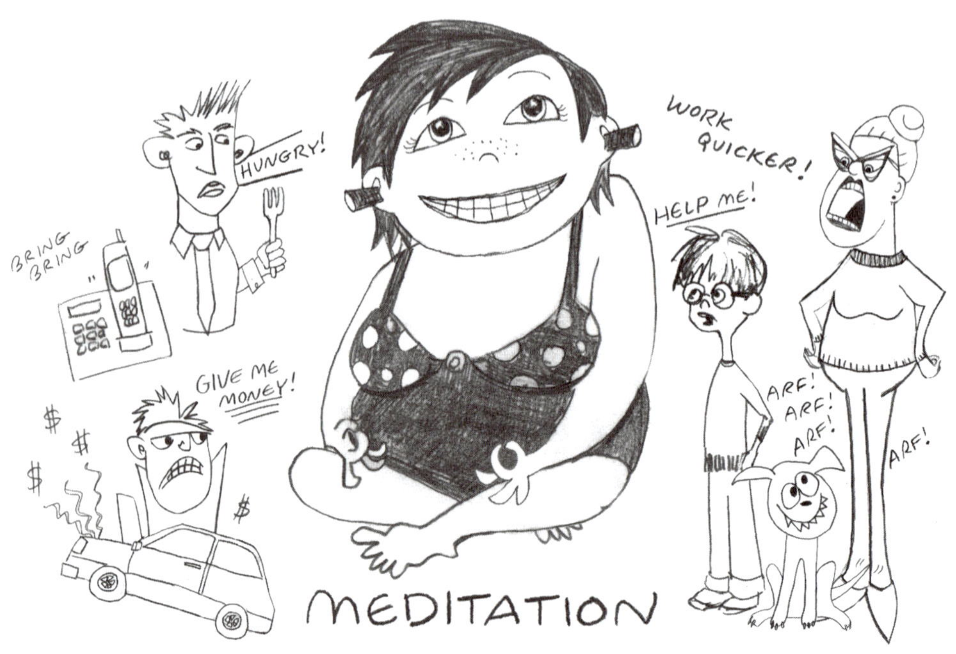

Introduction

Why People Draw

Drawing makes your brain happy.

When you draw, you are using multiple brain regions. Your frontal lobe kicks into action providing reasoning, planning, movement, emotions, and problem solving. Your parietal lobe provides movement and orientation, recognition, perception of stimuli; your occipital lobe delivers visual processing; your temporal lobe, perception and memory; and your cerebellum, additional movement.

When you draw, you are concentrating, allowing the rewarding neurotransmitter dopamine to flow. Some people report feelings of calm. Others say drawing allows them to keenly focus.

Drawing entertains many of us.

Drawing is a way to make sense of one's self in the world, a way to relate to others and to explore one's own identity. It allows you to explore what you see in the visible world and interpret what you see.

Drawing is a way to visually communicate ideas and feelings.

Drawing visually records people, places, things, memories, and events.

Drawing is a form of creative self-expression.

Drawing is visual thinking—a cognitive way to explore and understand ideas and experiences.

Drawing from observation entails interpreting and visualizing what you see. Or you might visualize what you think in a conceptual drawing, or you can visualize what you imagine.

As a child, tracing your hand was a magical way to replicate your hand. Instinctively you knew the drawing was a record of your existence. Now, drawing can be anything you desire: naturalistic, realistic, stylized, abstract, nonobjective, whimsical, satirical, flat, illusionistic, textural, colorful, expressionistic—anything.

This book introduces drawing topics in a logical way, allowing you to build technical and compositional skills and comprehension. Some techniques have comprehensive step-by-step instructions. Some instructions are short prompts that cue a creative action. Highly esteemed artists, designers, illustrators, architects, filmmakers, animators, cartoonists, educators, and other creative professionals contributed many of the prompts in this book.

There are many ways to draw. Portraying the world as we see it is only one way to visualize. This guided sketchbook will teach you how to draw what you see as well as encourage you to draw conceptually and experiment. So make your brain happy—draw!

B.E.S.T. Practice

When drawing, it's B.E.S.T. to:

Be patient. Breathe. Relax and enjoy yourself. Learning to draw takes time.

Erase. Feel free to make mistakes. All visual artists do.

Stay open to experimentation, which expands your vision and drawing vocabulary.

Toss out preconceived notions. Enter this experience freshly.

More Best Practice Tips to Remember

- Try to use "gist" thinking, or *big-picture thinking,* to think about the whole rather than parts. For example, when drawing a still life, don't render one object and then move on to the next. Rather, work the entire composition at the same time, cultivating spatial relationships.
- Play!
- Observe mindfully.
- Evaluate spatial relationships. Pay as much attention to the interstices—the spaces between forms—as to the forms themselves. Imagine that between each form in your drawing there is a stretchy band that creates visual tension.

Draw! Checklist

Have You S.E.E.N. It?

S = Spatial relationships. Consider the spaces between forms as much as the forms themselves.

E = Edges. Consider all drawn elements in response to the format's edges.

E = Emphasis. Consider emphasizing some elements and deemphasizing others. Create a focal point.

N = Negative shapes/space. Consider all negative space.

- ❐ Does the page's orientation best suit the direction or emphasis of your subject matter?
- ❐ What kind of graphic or pictorial space do you want to create? (Flat or illusory? Near or far?)
- ❐ Have you created a focal point?
- ❐ Have you arranged the composition to guide the viewer through the pictorial space?
- ❐ Have you created a point of entry into the composition?
- ❐ Have you evaluated spatial relationships?
- ❐ Did you consider the negative shapes?
- ❐ Is the composition balanced? (If not, what expressive purpose does imbalance serve?)
- ❐ Have you drawn with as much specificity to each shape or form as possible?
- ❐ Have you used tools to their best advantage?

Diamond Rivera

{ARTIST}

"When starting off with an idea and a blank page you don't need to tell every inch of the story. You need to include enough detail to allow the viewer to get an idea of what is going on.

"You can let them fill in some blanks, too, which will keep the audience engaged for a longer period of time. And it's OK if not everyone walks away with the same story.

"Crop your drawing to give it an interesting perspective."

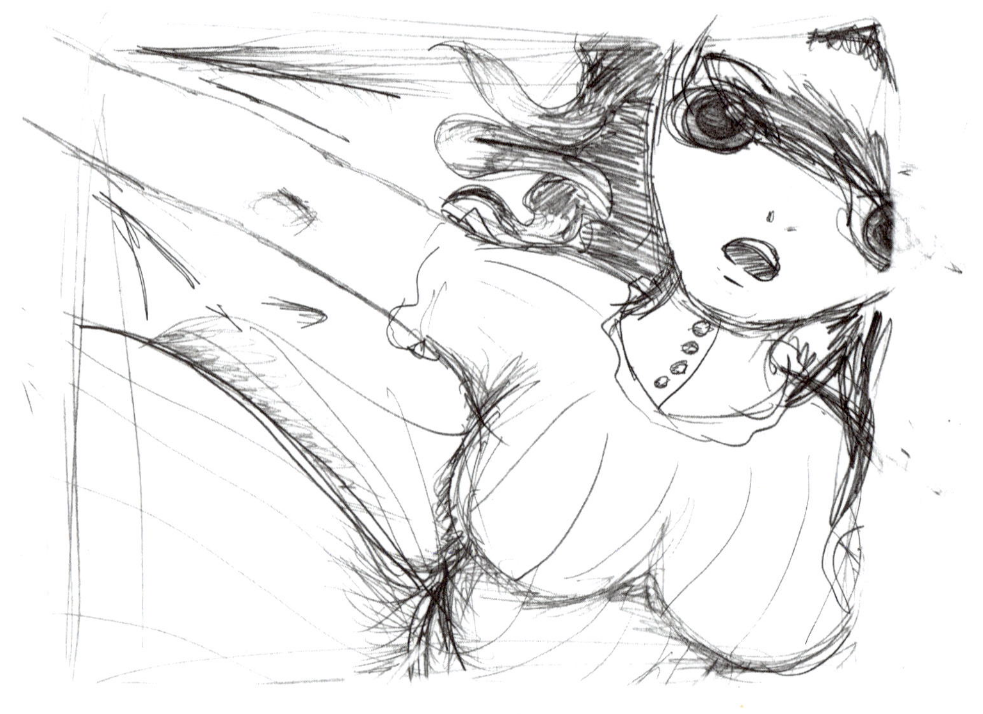

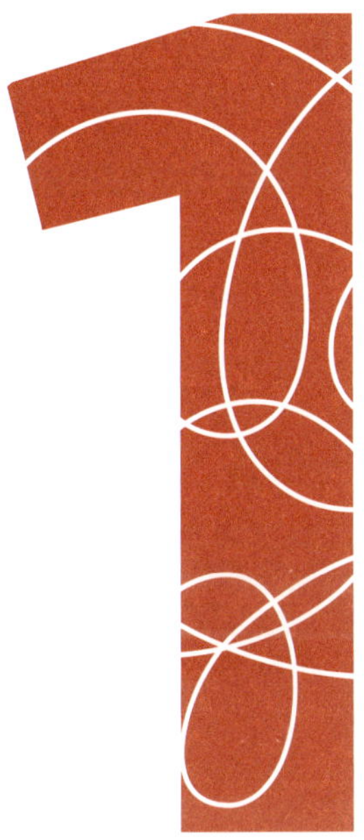

Visual Thinking

You can learn to draw more proficiently by being a keen observer. In this chapter, before you pick up a pencil, you'll learn how to take a closer look at the visual relationships all around you, and you'll start to see shapes you never noticed before. You'll be amazed at how sharp observation will improve your drawing skills and alter your perception of the world.

Think About the Page

Whether it's paper or digital, every page has a defined perimeter—its outer edges or boundaries—as well as the field it encloses. Consider what you're drawing and how the marks you make relate to the page's edges and outer shape.

Page Orientation Is Important

Paper and digital pages come in all shapes and sizes—rectangular, square, round, quadrilateral, and freeform. Orient your page to best suit the pictorial space you want to create and/or your subject matter. If you observe a vertical emphasis in the subject matter, position the page in a vertical orientation and vice versa.

Each element of your drawing will respond to the page's boundaries and shape. A page not only has all that white space ready to receive your first mark, but it also has edges that function as part of your composition.

If you draw a line parallel to one edge of a page, that line will echo the directional force of that side. Drawn lines that are *not* parallel generally are more visually active. For example, diagonal or curved lines drawn within a rectangle tend to be more active. If the shape of the page is elongated in one direction, lines parallel to the elongated side will be more forceful. If the page is circular, a curving line echoes the circumference, while horizontal, vertical, or angled lines differ from the round circumference, creating visual tension by moving in opposition to the circular boundary.

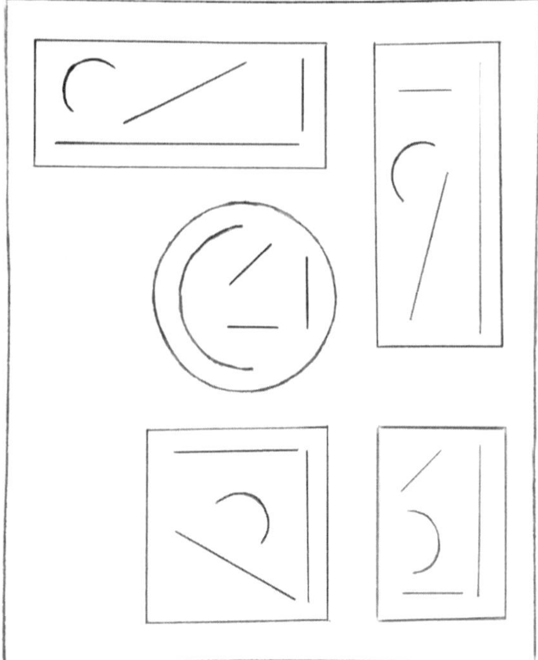

Diagram of movements in various shaped formats

A Page's Field Relates to Its Edges

As soon as you draw one mark on the blank page, you begin to build a composition within the internal graphic or pictorial space. (*Graphic space* and *pictorial space* can be used interchangeably, however, graphic space best describes nonrepresentational works and pictorial space best describes representational works.) Here are some things to think about as you start any drawing.

Closed and Open Compositions

A drawing can be closed (or tectonic) or open (a-tectonic). Let's start with a discussion of open composition.

When you draw, you can consider the page an *open* field. You can build a composition that seems to go on forever, defying and somehow dissolving the edges of the page, creating an *a-tectonic composition*.

Or you can consider the page's edges as hard and fast boundaries within which your composition is firmly contained or closed *(tectonic)*. Echoing the edges of the page in the composition reiterates the boundaries. In a closed composition, the marks or imagery appear held within. Often, in closed compositions, elements parallel the edges. Internal drawn elements respond to the edges but all action stops at the edges.

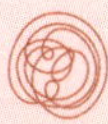

Try this: Look straight ahead at an object in the actual room space in front of you. As you are looking straight ahead, consider how the space moves beyond your focus into the outer part of your field of vision, into your peripheral vision. The boundaries of your vision aren't hard and fast but instead go on beyond your focus. This is what an open composition simulates.

Now try this: Focus intently on one object. That focus keeps you from moving to the periphery of your vision.

The terms *closed* and *open* refer to the way the drawn elements of a composition relate to the edges of a page. Basically, if the major movements within a composition oppose the edges (think diagonals) or direct our eyes past the boundaries of the format, that composition is considered open. If the internal imagery or marks' directions echo the page's edges to a great extent *and* the viewer's focus is kept tightly within the format, that composition is considered closed.

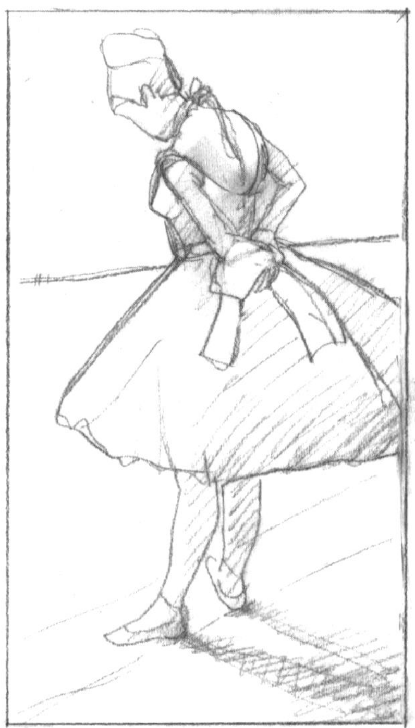

Closed and open compositions after Edgar Degas

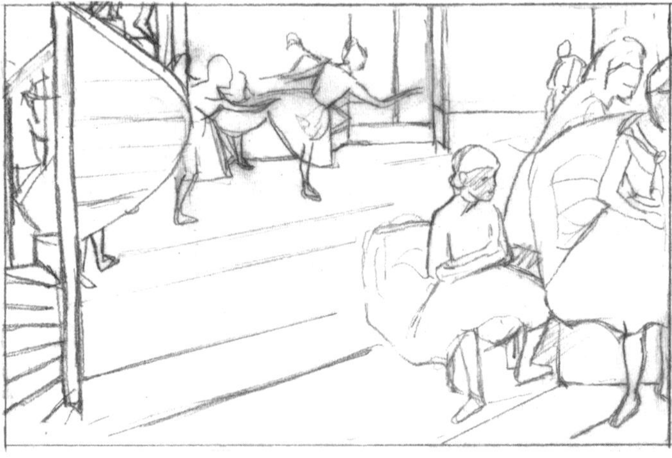

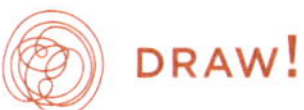

DRAW!

In these two rectangles, sketch a spiral or a rotating column that looks like a tornado. In one, compose a closed composition; sketch the tornado parallel to the vertical edges and keep the tornado clearly within the boundaries of the rectangle. In the other, compose an open composition by sketching the spiral so that it looks like the tornado is tilted and moving outside of the boundaries.

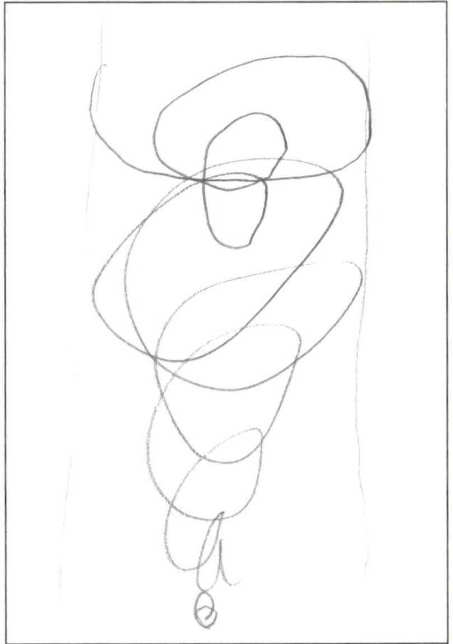

About Composition

If you've ever used a camera, you have composed a photograph. When you look through a camera's viewfinder, you compose what you see so that it is arranged aesthetically within the frame.

Drawing involves composing as well. You have to translate the three-dimensional space you observe or imagine onto a fixed two-dimensional surface. Most artists do not use a viewfinder to compose scenes from life, but some find it helpful. As you learn to draw from life, a viewfinder (a piece of clear acetate or plastic that is divided into a modular grid) is a handy tool, not just for composing a single composition but also for learning to *see the world within the confined format of a rectangle*. The edges of the viewfinder correspond to the edges of the paper, which allows you to see how the forms would be positioned in a composition. Some viewfinders are divided into modules based on the Rule of Thirds.

Rule of Thirds

The *Rule of Thirds* is a compositional technique often used by painters, photographers, and designers, although some never use it and still produce quality work. The technique uses asymmetry to create visual interest and balance. In practice, the aim of the Rule of Thirds is to prevent the placement of the focal point at the center of a composition or to discourage placements that divide the composition in half. Generally, placements that split a page in half act to divide a composition rather than create a focal point.

Here's how it works: A nine-module grid helps you to position the focal point or primary graphic elements of the composition along its grid lines, especially at the intersections of the grid lines. The focal point is placed at one intersection and a counterbalancing secondary pictorial element is placed at an opposing intersection. Also, a horizontal grid line could represent the horizon line in a landscape.

Although the intersections provide guidelines for the placement of primary elements, you still need to make judgments involving balance and counterpoint. After working with the Rule of Thirds as a guideline for a while, you will learn to compose with visual interest and can abandon this grid or a viewfinder.

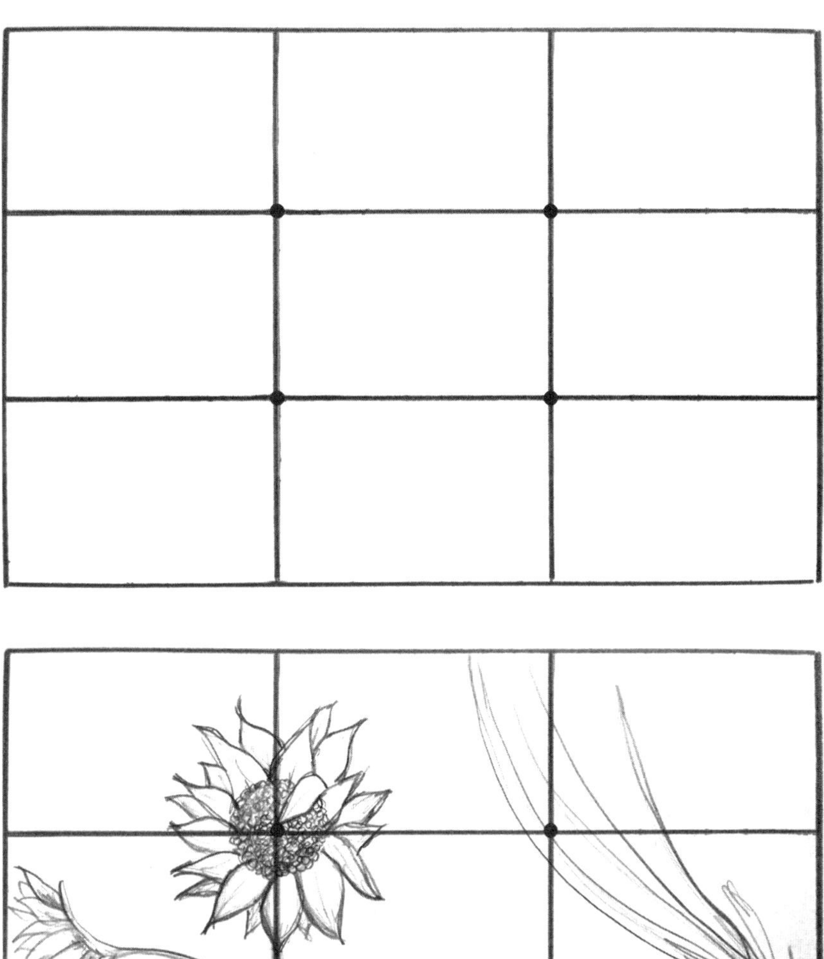

Drawing by Denyse Mitterhofer

The Rule of Thirds is sometimes called the *golden grid rule* because the modules created by the grid relate roughly to the ratio of the golden section (rule of thirds: 2/3 = 0.666; the golden section = 0.618). Throughout the history of Western art, artists, designers, and architects have used the golden section as a basis for proportions and dividing pictorial space. The golden section is a ratio; as an equation it is $(a + b)/a = a/b$. Many consider shapes or structures defined by or based on the golden section to be aesthetically pleasing.

Please note: You can successfully organize a composition with a centered focal point or even by dividing the composition in half: Just look at works by some of the great Italian painters of the Middle Ages, such as Duccio, or at images of the Mughal emperors in India by artists such as Govardhan. But for now, as you learn how to draw, you will benefit from learning how to organize asymmetrical compositions. Just remember that each composition must be evaluated independently for aesthetic merit and for how the basic principles of composition are employed.

The Picture Plane

Any page—a piece of paper or a screen—is a two-dimensional surface, a *plane*. The *picture plane* is the blank, flat, two-dimensional surface of a page. As soon as you make one mark (draw a line, a letterform, a stroke of color, or a scribble) on the surface, that mark affects the appearance and graphic position of the picture plane (*and* reacts to the perimeter of the page's edges).

Foreground, Middle Ground, and Background

In any drawing, the picture plane can be manipulated to create the illusion of spatial depth. There are three key planes:

- The *foreground* is the part of a composition that appears nearest the viewer;
- The *middle ground* is an intermediate position between the foreground and the background; and
- The *background* is what appears in the distance or lies behind the most important pictorial or graphic elements in the composition.

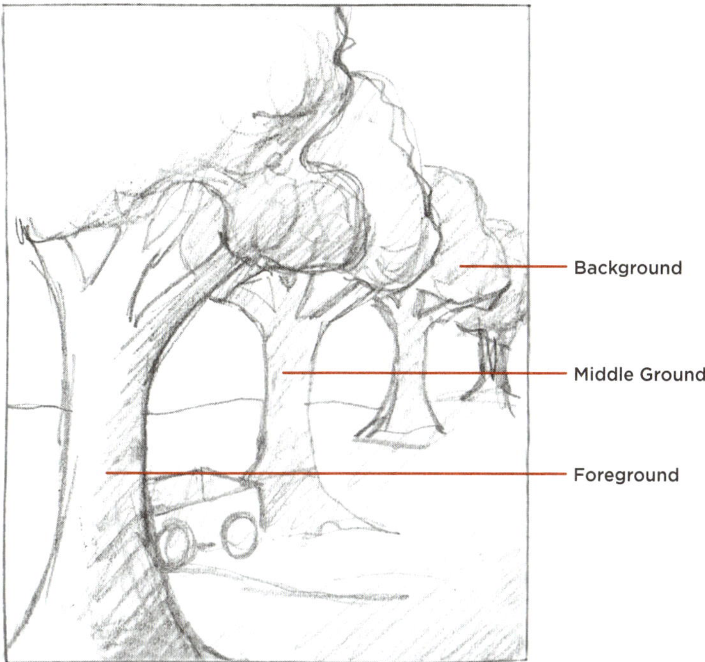

To create the illusion of three-dimensional space, pictorial or graphic elements positioned in the foreground are bigger and/or brighter, may be rendered in greater detail, and have more contrast than those in the middle ground and background. This (conventional Western) pictorial illusion of space on a two-dimensional surface imitates the way we perceive forms in the real world: Forms appear to become smaller and grayer as they move away from us and recede into the distance.

Observing Visual Relationships

Most likely, when you read the word "apple," a mental image comes into your mind. But when you look at an apple with the intention of drawing it, you must turn away from the idea of an apple, that picture in your mind, and instead turn to careful observation of the apple sitting before you. *This is one of the most important takeaways from this book.*

What is the specific shape and form of the apple? What are the specific colors? Where is it in space? How big is it in relation to other objects around it? Is light falling on it? Can you translate its three-dimensional mass as well as shape onto a two-dimensional surface? (The more you draw from life, carefully observing what you see, the easier it will be to draw from memory.)

Visual Reckoning

Say you want to draw an apple and a vase on a tabletop. To represent these items in a drawing, you first have to make comparisons between and among forms, which you can think of as *visual reckoning*.

There are many factors to consider before you begin to draw. Start with these simple questions:

- Which object is bigger? How much smaller is one than the other?
- How tall is the apple in relation to the vase?
- How wide is one compared to the other? Compared to the table?
- What are the length, width, and depth of the apple? Vase? Table?
- How much space on the page will they occupy?

Sighting

You can employ what is called *sighting* to determine the relative heights and widths as well as angles of the forms in your subject matter.

Use your pencil as a measuring tool to compare relative heights and widths. Close one eye. Holding your pencil, extend your arm straight out. Align the tip of the pencil with the top of an object and use your thumb to indicate the end of the object. Keeping your thumb to that measurement on the pencil, compare it to the size of another form in the room space, still life, or landscape.

To determine the slant of an angle, you employ a similar procedure. Close one eye. Holding your pencil, extend your arm out. Turn your pencil to match the angle. Compare it to other angles or to straight edges. Translate it to your drawing.

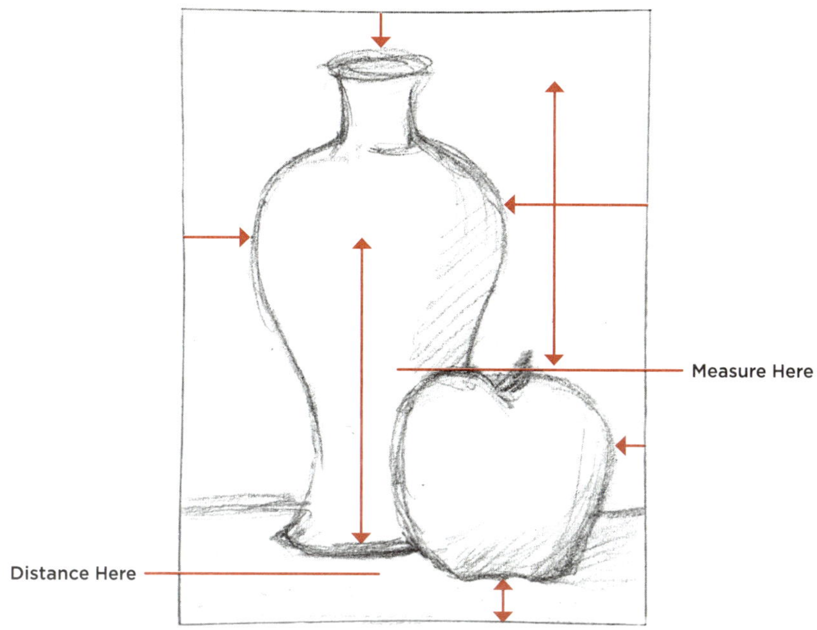

Study Overlaps and Interstices

- Are the objects next to one another or do they overlap? If they overlap, which one is in front? How much do they overlap? (Overlaps create the illusion of depth.)
- Visually approximate the distances between and among objects; judge *interstices* (spaces between forms).
- If there are spaces between the objects, what shapes do the spaces make?
- Are the objects positioned close to the front edge of the table? Close to the rear of the table? Near a wall? Where are objects and figures in a room? At the front of the room?

Observing Visual Relationships

In order to interpret and portray what you see in the real world on a flat surface, you make determinations. You are not literally going to measure anything with a ruler, but you are going to do some *visual reckoning,* keenly observing visual relationships. You might:

- Visually calculate dimensions such as the size (length, width, and depth) and the scale of objects in relation to one another.
- Judge the overall shape and/or form of each object. Is it a circle or sphere? Is it circular or an ellipse? Rectangular or square? Square or a cube?
- Understand proportions of an individual object or figure as well as its proportions in relation to other forms.
- Visually measure distances among objects and interstices.
- Observe negative spaces (shapes), that is, the spaces that do not contain imagery.
- Read light and shadow.
- Notice color.
- Determine a point of view (where you are in relation to the subject matter—directly in front, to a side, above, or below, as well as whether you are close or far away).
- Analyze views for foreshortening (to shorten a form in the direction of depth to create the illusion of projection or extension in space).

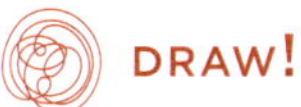

Position a few items from your kitchen or office on a tabletop. Overlap some of them. Note their respective heights and how they overlap.

Look out of a window. Keenly observe overlapping objects. Is there a tree in front of a car? If so, what is their visual relationship? How tall are the objects in relation to one another?

Draw one object overlapping another. Did you create the illusion of spatial depth by drawing one object overlapping another?

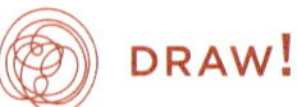

Part 1: Look out into the space of the room you are in. Draw only the shape that space makes between two objects in the room (for example, the space between a chair and a table).

Part 2: Place your nondrawing hand on your hip and observe yourself in a mirror. Draw the shape of the space created between your arm and your torso.

Part 3: Stand in front of a full-length mirror. Bend one leg, placing the foot of the working leg on the part of the standing leg between the base of the calf and the beginning of the ankle, what is called a *sur le cou-de-pied* (on the neck of the foot) in ballet. Observe the shape of the resulting space. Return to your book to draw the shape of the space you observed.

Determine a Point of View

Where are you standing in relation to the objects you see? What is your point of view? Do you see them in full view? Do you see things from a side view or at an angle? Do you see anything in a foreshortened view?

Read Light and Shadow

Is light falling on the objects? Is it falling from one side? Top? Bottom? Are there shadows on the objects? Are there cast shadows on the tabletop or floor?

Read Color

Which colors (hues, values, and chromatic intensities) do you see? Are the colors warm or cool?

Eyeballing and Perspective

Most drawing courses include learning perspective, a schematic way of translating three-dimensional space onto a two-dimensional surface. Perspective is based on the idea that diagonals moving toward a point on the horizon, called the *vanishing point,* will imitate the recession of space into the distance and create the illusion of spatial depth. Italian Renaissance artist and architect Filippo Brunelleschi, who had reproduced a three-dimensional object in two dimensions, is credited with inventing perspective.

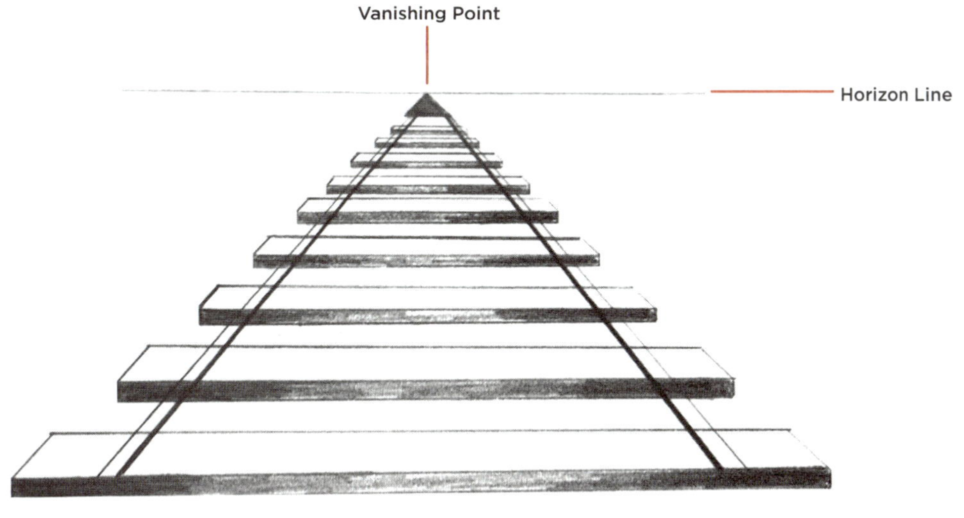

Most artists and designers create the illusion of spatial depth with less formal methods, by "eyeballing" what they see or imagine rather than using official perspectival drawing methods. We'll begin with learning to draw what we see by eyeballing, by astute observations.

Essentially, when your intent is to create a pictorial space that imitates what you see in the world, you need to understand this: That small sketchbook page you hold in your hands becomes the framing unit of an illusion of three-dimensional space. The page becomes a field of vision. If you want figures to look like they are standing on the ground, you must think about creating a tilted floor plane for them to stand on. If you want pictorial space to look like it is receding into the distance, you must think about the sizes of elements—the scale of things in relation to one another and to the page.

Flat or with Depth?

You can conjure the illusion of three-dimensional space in a drawing, denying the characteristic flatness of the paper or screen. That illusion of space can be shallow, deep, ambiguous, or even fractured (think Cubism). Or you can maintain the flatness of the page in a drawing. It's completely up to you.

Shading and tone create the illusion of volume, too. We will cover this topic in Chapters 5 and 6.

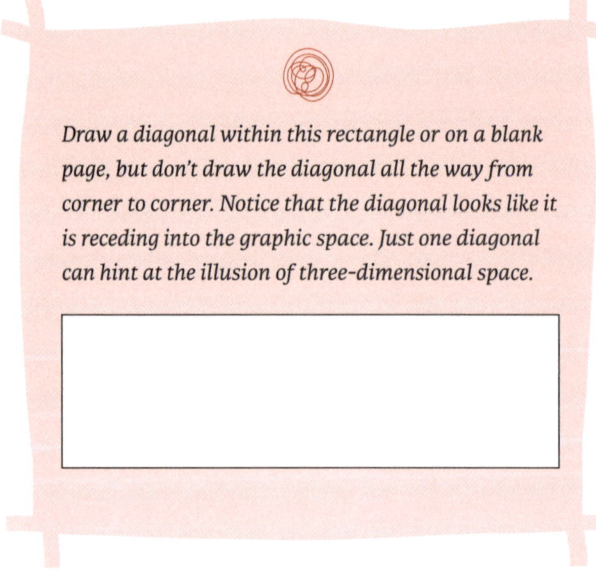

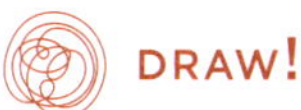

Draw a simple room space on this page, like the one you see in the diagram. Add a few objects, such as a cube, a chair, or a figure, to create the illusion of three-dimensional forms in space.

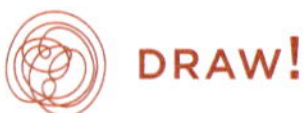

Sketch a person with rearranged body parts, facial features, or both.

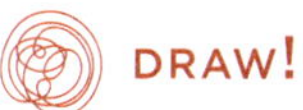

"There are a few classic life-drawing techniques that my drawing professor Robert Cimbalo used that come to mind...

"Tape or tie the drawing implement to a long stick and draw with it. This hones sensitivity to gesture and composition. Or draw with the same, but using the opposite hand. Or just draw with the unextended tool but with the opposite hand. Amazingly enough, often the drawings done with the 'wrong' hand may be better and more interesting realizations of the subject."
—James Romberger, Artist

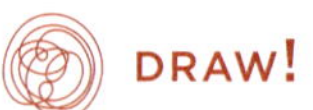

"Buy yourself some flowers, or even better, have someone else give you flowers, then draw them; something I just did recently. (I was given some carnations.)"
—Polly Apfelbaum, Artist

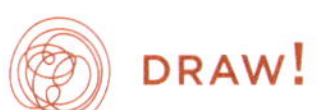

"Draw your childhood home from memory, then go to Google maps and see if it is anything like you remember."
—James Gulliver Hancock, Illustrator, www.jamesgulliverhancock.com

Hsinping Pan

{ANIMATOR, WWW.HSINPINGPAN.COM}

"Imagine yourself as a plant; give the plant your personality and draw some plant friends too."

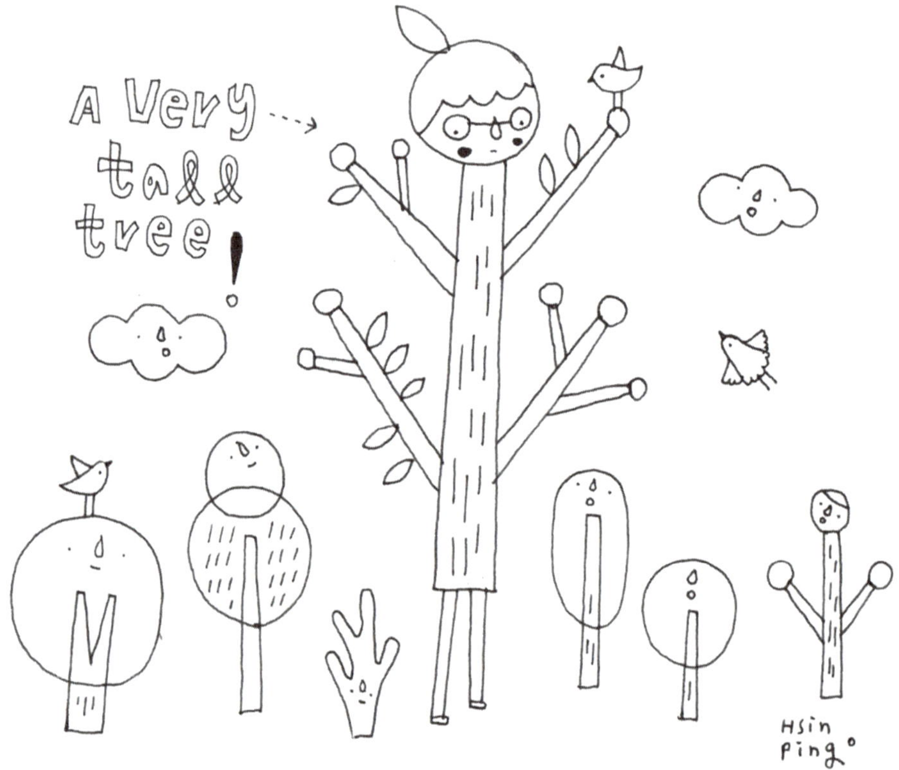

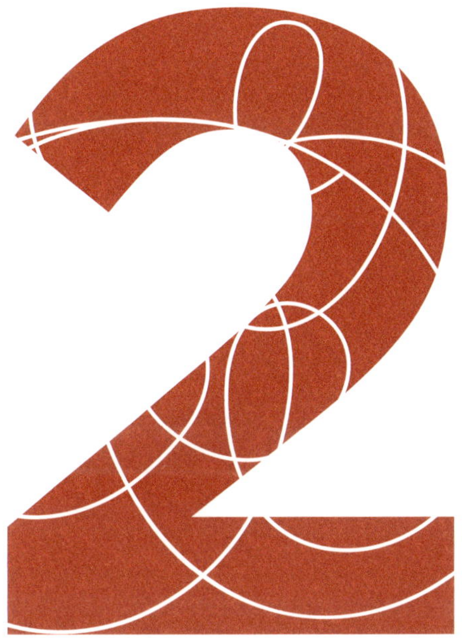

The Formal Elements of Drawing

Whether you draw a line made with a celery stalk dipped in ink or your reliable pencil, you're creating a versatile yet fundamental visual element—*line*. Use line to draw a pineapple and you've created a *shape*. Add *tone, color, texture* or *pattern* to that image of a pineapple, and you're employing the other formal elements of fine art and design to develop your drawing. Each element contributes to expression. Drawing landscapes, faces, or anything from your imagination or observation demands an exploration of each of these formal elements.

Line

Hold a pen in your hand and move it across a page. You drew a line. Draw the letter "S". That's a curved line. Dip your finger in chocolate sauce and draw a lightning bolt on your arm. That's a line, too.

A line is the path of a moving point—a mark made by a drawing tool as it is drawn across a surface. You can draw a line with a variety of tools, such as a pencil, a marker, a pointed brush, a digital pen, or any other object that can make a mark, even with a rosebud dipped in soy sauce.

Pick up a pencil and draw a line. That line will have direction and quality. Lines can be straight, curved, or angular. They can guide the viewer's eyes in a direction or path. Whether delicate or bold, smooth or broken, thick or thin, regular or changing, a line has a specific quality.

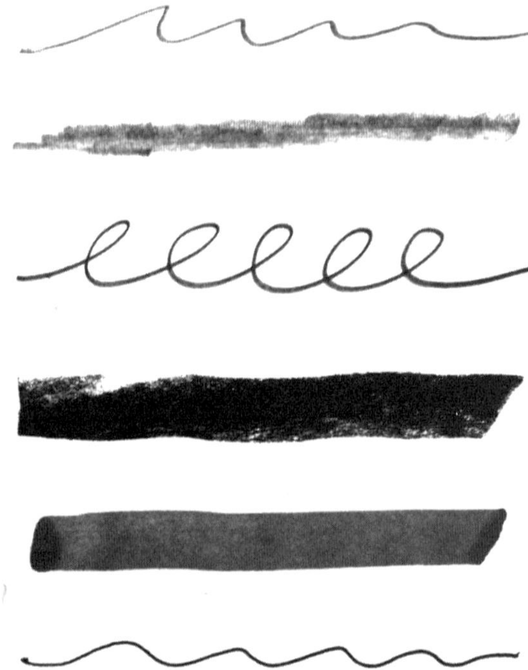

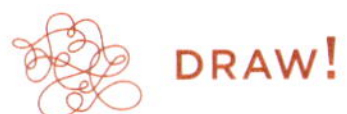

DRAW!

Draw a solid line that moves playfully across the page.

Draw an implied line: a broken (noncontinuous) line. Break it just enough so that the viewer still *perceives* the broken line to be continuous.

Draw two shapes that share a boundary, for example, two triangles that share a side.

Draw a line that will guide the movement of a viewer's eyes in a specific direction. For example, draw a sweeping line that clearly moves from top to bottom.

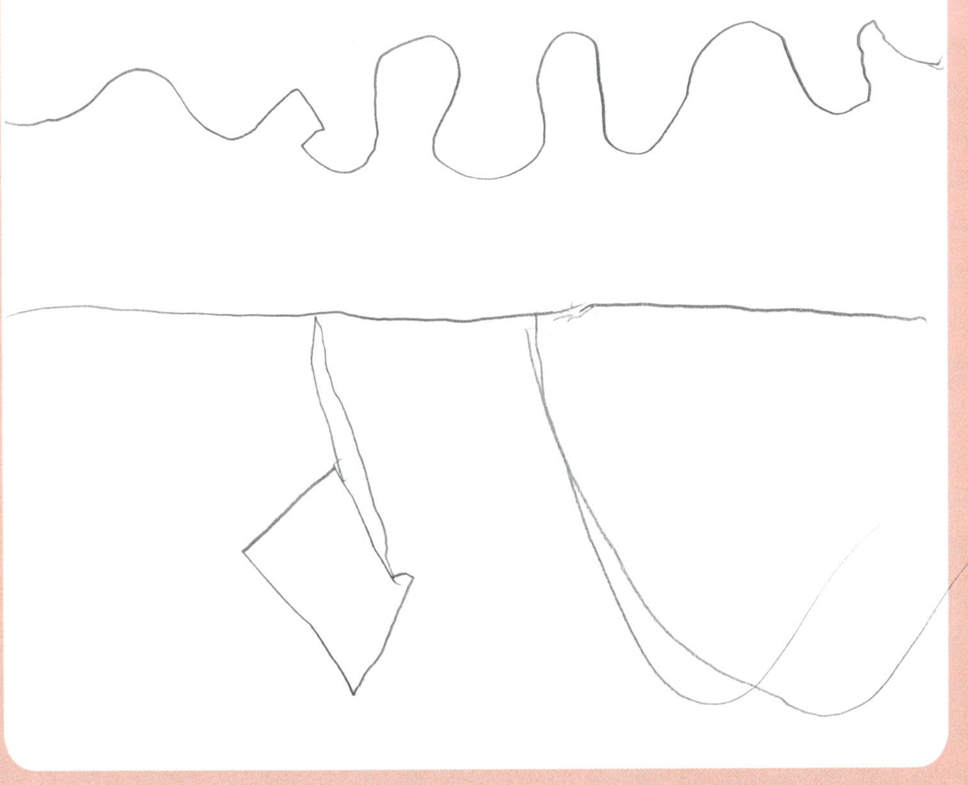

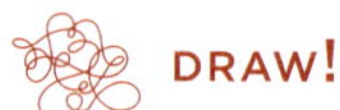

DRAW!

Find a cable or cord, such as an iPhone earbud cord or a charging cable. Use the cable as a "line," arranging it in an interesting configuration. Draw the configuration on this page, engaging the entire page. (For an observational challenge, arrange a complex configuration and try drawing it from memory.)

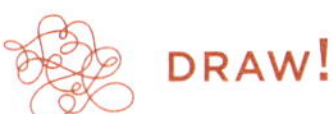

DRAW!

Close your eyes and imagine a real or fantastic creature or object, such as an octopus, a dragon, or a bridge. Using only line, draw the outline of it. Draw the creature or object big enough to touch at least three sides of the page.

Shape

When you prefer one car model over another, shape factors into your decision. It's the same for choosing a mate. You may not think about how the shape of something (or someone) factors into your selections but it often does. A shape is the general outline of an object, figure, or form. It also is defined as a closed form or closed path. You can draw a shape by using lines (for outlines and contours) or by using color, tone, or texture.

A shape is flat. Essentially, all shapes may be derived from three basic delineations: the square, the triangle, and the circle. Each of these basic shapes has a corresponding volumetric form or mass: the cube, the pyramid, and the sphere.

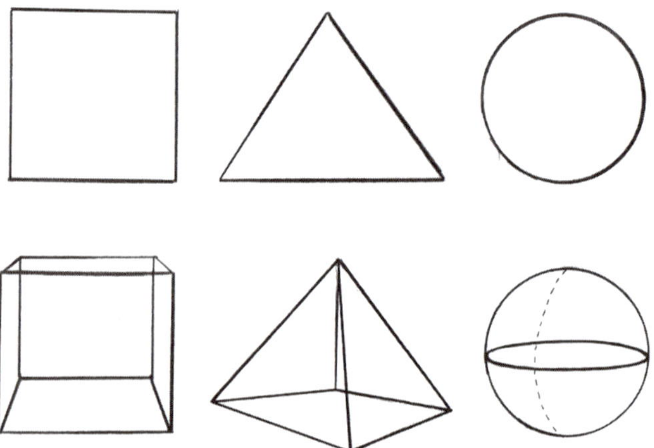

Figure/Ground

Picture your friend striking a wild pose with outstretched limbs in front of a blank wall. Your friend is the *figure* and the wall is the *ground* (or background). Most likely, in that wild pose your friend's limbs visually divide the wall into some interesting shapes, which are called *negative shapes*.

Another example: The type you're reading on this page is the figure or positive shapes. The white page is the ground (or remaining negative graphic space).

Whether you're considering the relationship of your friend to the wall or type to the page its on, each pair has a figure/ground (or positive/negative) shape relationship. The average person might consider the background or negative shapes as "leftover" but *a visual artist must always consider the shape relationship between the figure and ground as an integral part of the composition*. No shape is leftover—consider all positive and negative shapes as active contributors to your composition.

Value

Choose light blue denim over dark blue denim. Paint the walls of your dining room light green rather than dark green. Create a palette of all dark colors instead of light colors. In each case, you've made a decision concerning value. *Value* refers to the level of luminosity—lightness or darkness—of a color, such as *light* blue or *dark* red.

In drawing, *value contrast* is most useful for purposes of differentiating shapes and forms. Note the value contrast of the type (the figure) and white paper (the ground) on the page you are now reading. This particular value contrast most clearly differentiates the figure from the ground.

Different value relationships produce different effects, both visual and expressive. A narrow range of values is called *low contrast* and it presents a quiet or subtle relationship that usually evokes a different emotional response from a viewer than a bolder wide range of values, which is referred to as *high contrast*.

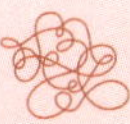

Black and white are colors (pigment), but they are not considered hues, like red or green. They are not *found on the visible spectrum and so are considered* achromatic *or* neutral *(without hue). Black is the darkest value and white is the lightest. Mixed together, black and white make gray. Grays are the interval neutral colors between black and white.*

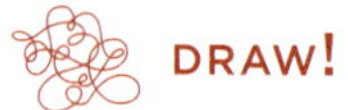

DRAW!

Give shapes some characteristics. Can you assign a "personality" to each shape's defining feature?

- Draw a geometric shape characterized by straight edges, precise curves, and/or measurable angles.
- Draw a curvilinear, organic, or biomorphic shape, formed by curves or flowing edges. Sketch it loosely or draw it precisely.
- Draw a rectilinear shape composed of straight lines or angles.
- Draw an irregular shape—a combination of straight and curved lines.
- Draw a nonrepresentational shape that you invent—that is, it doesn't literally represent a person, place, or known thing.

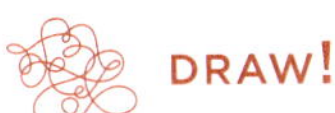

DRAW!

1. Inscribe a pear shape in one rectangle. The pear is the figure. The remaining background space is the ground. What would happen to the graphic space if you drew lots of squiggles in the background? Try it.
2. Draw a big star in the other rectangle so that the points of the star touch each of the four sides. The star is the figure and the remaining triangular shapes are negative shapes. Would the triangles appear more active if you added color to them? Try it.

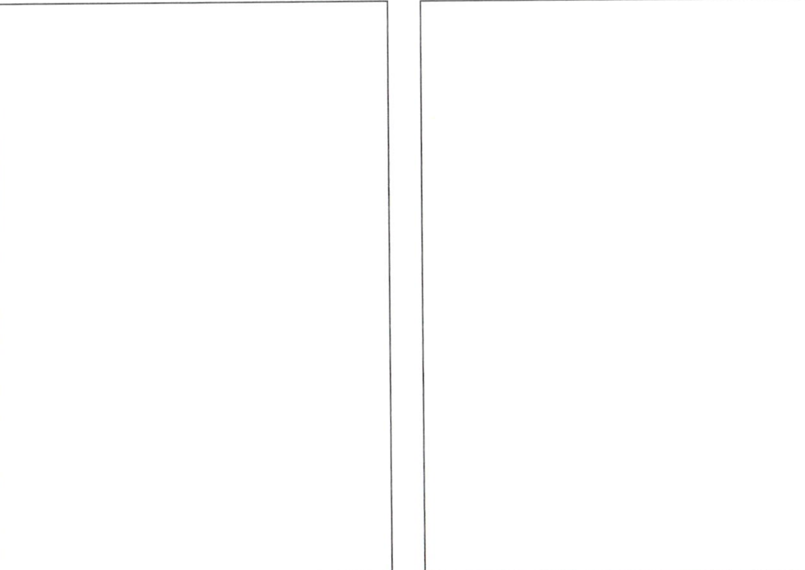

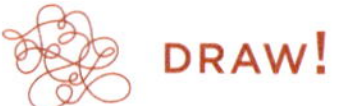

DRAW!

Fill one entire rectangle with a really thick letter "N". Do you see two triangles in the background—one at the top and one at the bottom?

In the other rectangle, create the letter "N" by drawing *only* the two triangles that form the negative shapes your previous "N" has on the top and bottom of it. You're forming the "N" by drawing the two negative shapes. (Visit moma.org to see *The Big N* by American painter Al Held.)

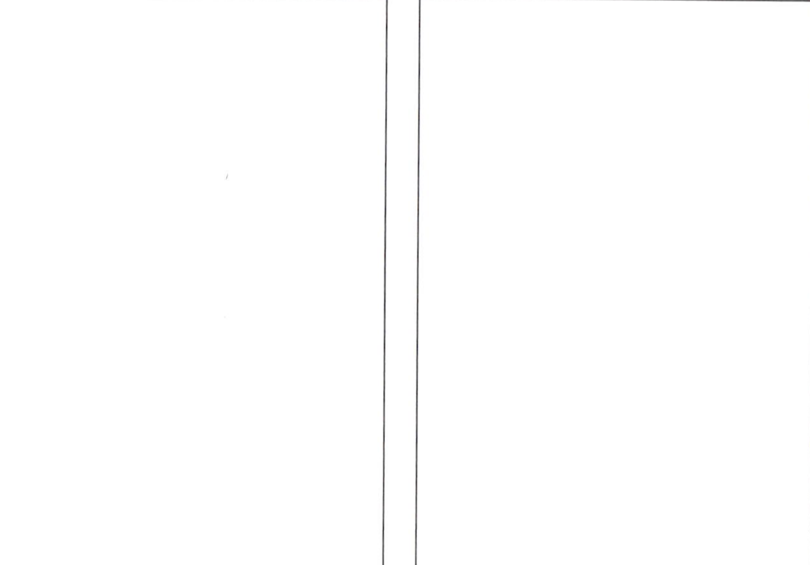

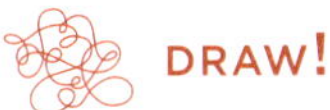

DRAW!

1. Draw the letter "X" in one square so that it touches the top and bottom.
2. Go over the "X" to make it thick. Do you see four white triangles in the background?
3. In the other square, draw four black triangles to form a letter "X." Don't draw the letter itself, please.

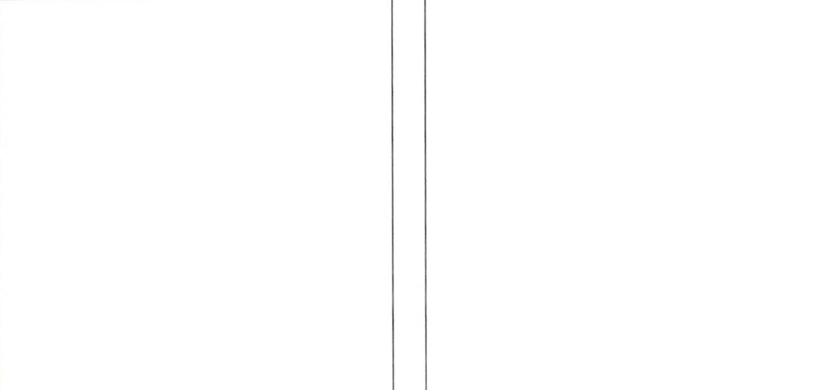

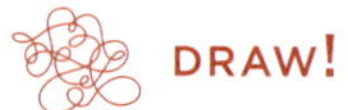

DRAW!

"Close your eyes and draw a ladderback chair from memory. Color in any negative spaces."
—Alexander Isley, Designer, Alexander Isley Inc.

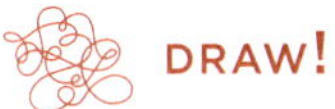

DRAW!

Find two keys, leaves, or two objects with interesting silhouettes. Position them on a tabletop. Note the negative space between the two objects and study its shape carefully. If the space between—an interstice—doesn't look interesting, rearrange the objects to yield something more intriguing. Draw the negative shape of the space between the two objects. Finally, draw the objects themselves.

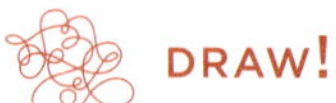

DRAW!

"Draw the negative space between your arm and body, ear and shoulder, your hip and chest, and in between your thighs."
—Lorin Latarro, Choreographer

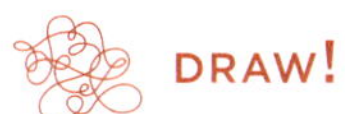

DRAW!

Sketch a leafy plant by drawing only the shapes between the leaves.

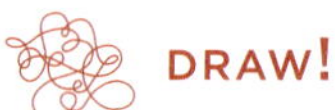

DRAW!

Sketch the outline of three bananas. Position one in the foreground, one in the middle ground, and one in the background. Color the one in the foreground solid black. Using either a gray marker, soft pencil, or vine charcoal, color the one in the middle gray. Leave the one in the background unfilled. Does adding value contrast increase the illusion of depth?

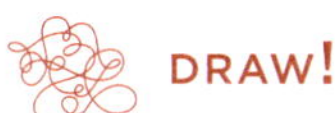

DRAW!

Sketch a box so that you can see some of its top plane. Use value contrast to create a greater illusion of three-dimensional form. Leave the front plane of the box blank. Make the top plane gray. Make the side plane black.

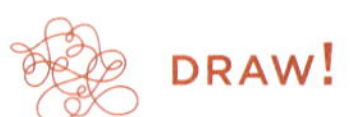

DRAW!

Using a soft pencil or vine charcoal, shade this area from light to dark with escalating shades of gray in between.

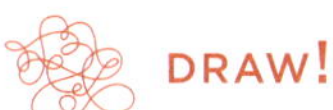

Fill this page with huge stars. Use a high contrast value scheme: Leave the stars white. Using a black marker or 6B pencil or black ink, fill in the negative spaces with black.

Color

How would you describe the color of pressed grapes? Or the color of dusk in autumn? Which green do you prefer? Visual artists and designers discuss *color* using three terms to accurately describe and specify it.

- *Hue* is the name of a color—red or green, for example.
- The *value* of a color is the lightness or darkness of a hue, such as *light* red or *dark* green.
- The brightness or dullness of a hue is called *saturation* or *intensity* or *chroma*—for example, *saturated* (bright) orange or *low-chroma* (dull) blue.

Texture

A chinchilla's fur beckons you to touch it. Rusty metal might not. *Texture* tempts our sense of touch—it is the tactile quality of a surface or the representation of such a surface. Tactile or actual textures have real tactile quality and can be physically touched and felt.

Visual textures are illusions of real textures created by hand, scanned from actual textures (such as lace), or photographed. You can learn to draw many different visual textures.

Pattern

In an instant, a *pattern* creates a visual language in which repetition and rhythm collaborate. A pattern can be an object of meditation, iconographic, a graphic visual field, or anything you fancy.

A pattern relies on a rigid repetition of a motif methodically organized within a given field. The motif can be any single shape or form—a dot, a line, a squiggle, a letterform, or a representational image such as a daisy or shirt—or a combination of shapes and/or forms as a unit. You can repeat the motif in four basic rigid ways:

- Repeats, in which the motif is repeated over and over again along horizontal and vertical axes;
- Half drop repeats, in which every other line of the motif is staggered;

- Rotation, when the original motif is coupled with a flipped version of itself; and
- Reflection, when the original motif is mirrored across an axis.

Patterns of parallel lines create stripes, while intersecting units of lines yield a pattern grid.

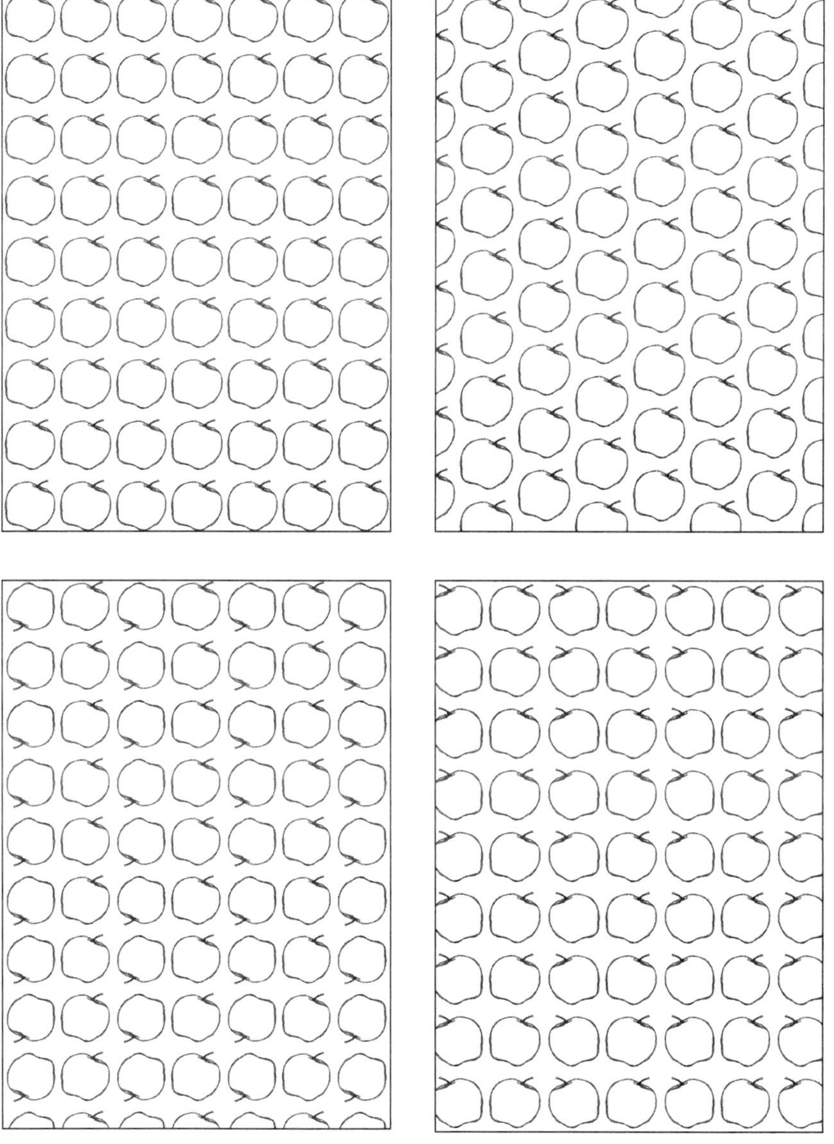

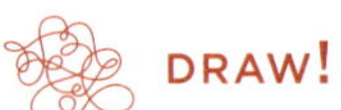

DRAW!

In each module of this grid, inscribe a different shape, for instance, a hammer or heart. Assign an emotion to each shape. Fill in each shape with one or more colors to communicate the specific emotion.

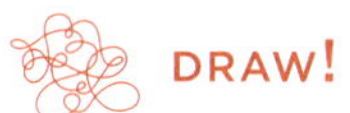

DRAW!

"Take yellow and make it the deepest, darkest color, incorporating it into a composition."
—Barbara Nessim, Artist, Illustrator and Educator

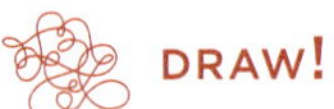

DRAW!

In each box, simulate a visual texture.

- Draw vertical lines over horizontal lines to simulate the texture of a window screen.
- Draw short curled lines to simulate the texture of hair.
- Draw tiny groups of open circles to look like Styrofoam.
- Draw small groups of five short, semicurved lines to simulate a woven fabric.

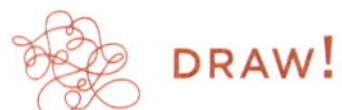

"Using the side of a charcoal, crayon, chalk, or pastel stick, combine rubbings of a variety of textured surfaces to create a textural mosaic."
—Shell Redfern, Program Manager, Design Studies, Southwest Florida College

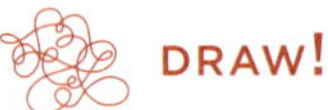

Create a simple pattern.

Step 1: Start with a series of dots or dashes drawn in a horizontal row.

Step 2: Add on. For example, draw a small rectangle around each dot or dash.

Step 3: Next, draw a teardrop or star shape under or above each rectangle.

Step 4: Repeat the row exactly or invert it.

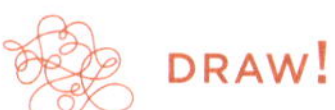

Doodling is a great way to learn about patterns. Start by drawing a continuous line around the page that intersects itself at several points. The intersections will divide this page into sections.

Create a palette of patterns, one used for each section. For example, one pattern could be based on triangles, another on a checkerboard pattern, another on bricks, another made of hatched lines changing direction or a woven straw basket pattern. Each patterned section contributes to the entire composition, built one pattern at a time.

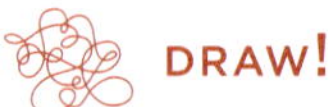

"Step on your sketch paper with your foot. Find and draw the pattern created (or make one up)."
—Jim Dawkins, Architect, Designer, Educator

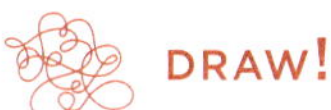

DRAW!

Using a black ballpoint pen, draw a pattern on a banana skin. Then press it onto this page.

Yoom Thawilvejakul

{ARTIST, WWW.FACEBOOK.COM/YOOMARTIST}

"Create surreal characters inspired by real objects."

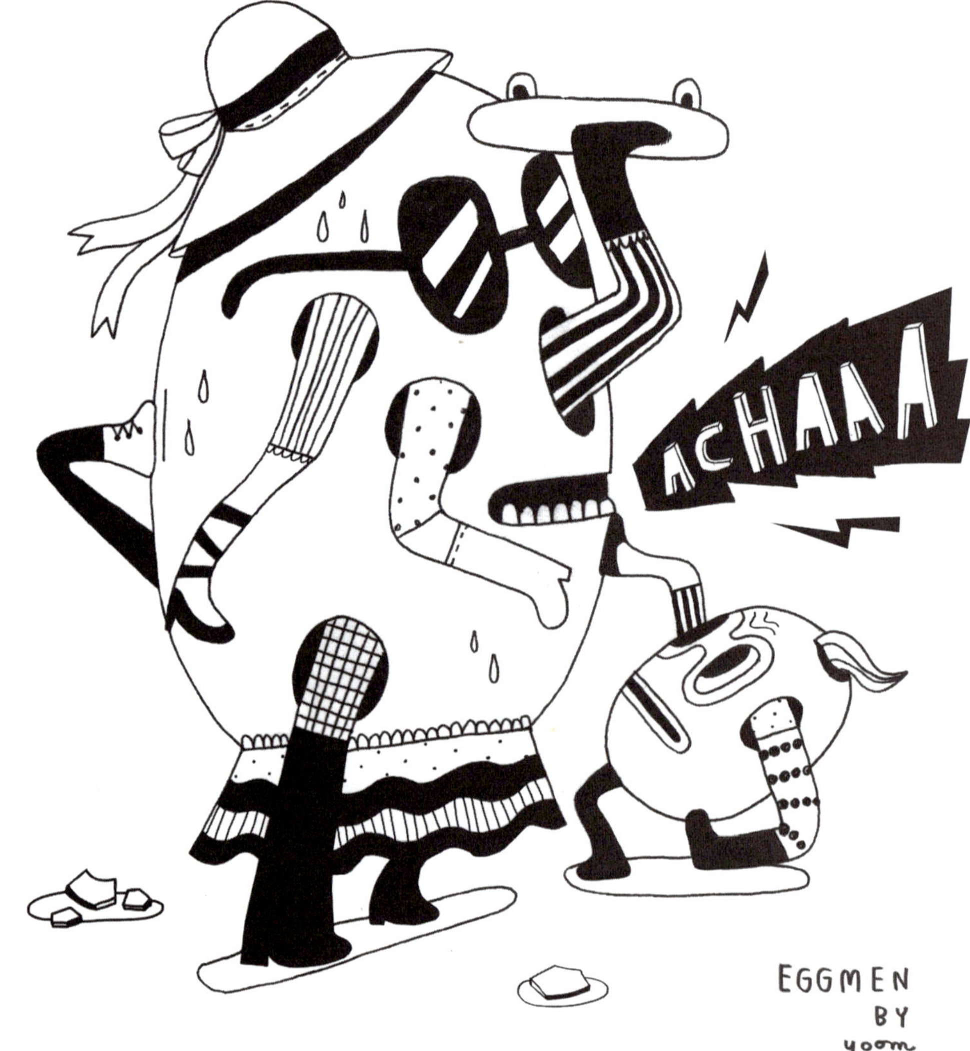

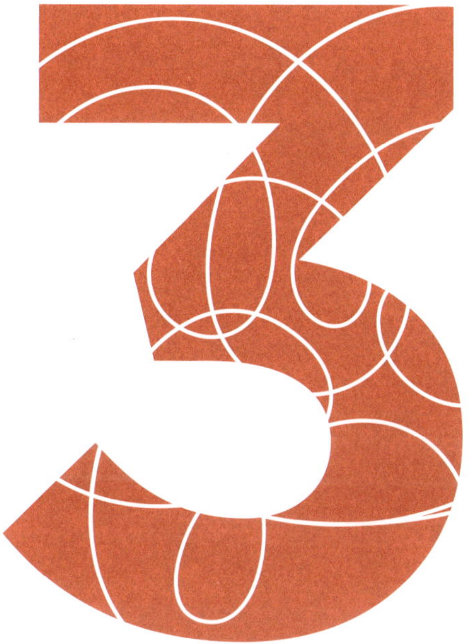

Compose!

Cars, birds, flora, real and imagined creatures, planes, dresses, cartoon characters, superheroes and villains, and more—people enjoy drawing what they love. They undertake the challenge of creating realism, carefully trying to render the full nature of what they see, including mass, texture, and perhaps color.

When you study drawing from life, you will soon learn that objects and figures have to exist somewhere in pictorial space. They are parts of a larger composition. That sets up a challenging visual thinking problem: When drawing from life, which should come first—drawing forms or composing the drawing?

Let's approach it this way: Think about something that you would like to draw. Where would it exist in actual space, out in the world? Now think about where it would exist in your drawing. Would it be in the foreground? Surrounded by nature? Flying through the air? Standing on the horizon?

So which comes first: drawing or composing? In truth, they need to happen at the same time, and learning to think this way will take some practice. This chapter will introduce some mind-bending exercises that will help you learn to draw the forms you want to create and place them in a drawn world with the proper spatial relationships.

How to Draw a Form

Anyone can plainly see that a soda can or tree trunk is cylindrical. Can you think of a human thigh or forearm as a cylindrical form as well? Could a man's chest be visualized as an upside-down cone? Could a soup bowl be formed from half of a sphere? Could an apartment building be constructed from a stack of cubes? Could you go so far as to think of a head as a cube?

On a flat page, you can draw an object or figure that appears to have mass. You can create the illusion of three-dimensional form. This can be done by using elemental forms: a sphere, a cube, a pyramid, a cone, a prism, or a cylinder. The trick is to train your vision to reduce objects to these basic forms.

Of course, the best way to learn to draw these basic forms is to look at them and draw what you observe. Learning how to sketch these forms will quickly enhance your general skills.

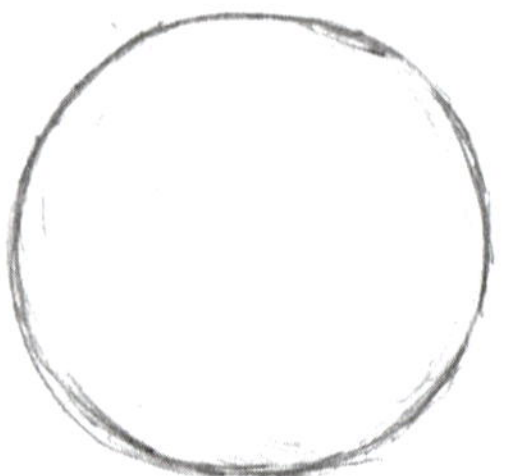
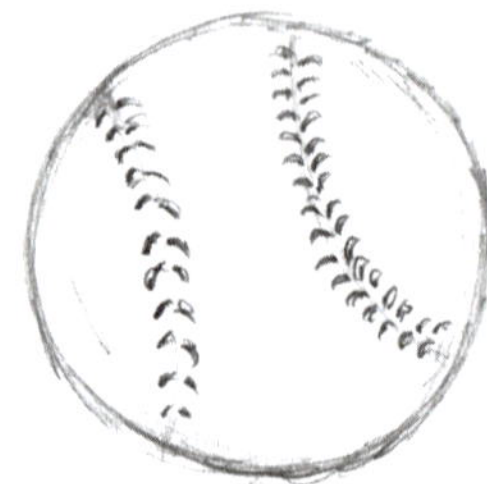
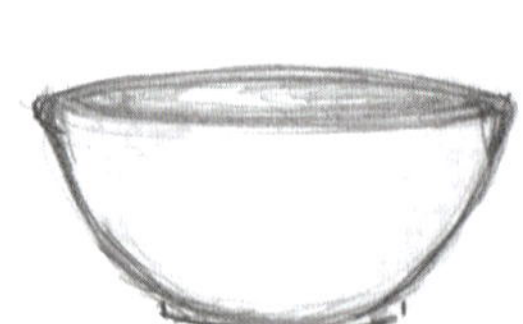

To draw a sphere, begin by using a soft pencil (6B) to draw a circle.

Partially erase the upper-left side of the circle, leaving an uneven line which should give the appearance of volume. Or:

- Draw a circle.
- Draw two straight lines dividing the circle into quarters.
- Draw ovals made of dashes around each line.
- Erase the original dividing lines.

The circle should begin to appear as a round, solid form, a sphere. Draw a line under the sphere to denote a floor or tabletop. Or turn it into a planet in outer space.

To draw a cube, start with a square shape.

- About half of the way down, draw another square overlapping the first square.
- Connect the four corners.
- Draw a horizonal line to denote the surface it is sitting on.

To draw a pyramid, begin by drawing a triangle.

- Next, draw a diagonal line from the tip of the triangle leaning to the right that ends before the bottom horizontal line.
- Connect the bottom-right corner to the end of the diagonal. What you did was create another narrower triangle attached to the right side of the first triangle.
- Shade the recessive side (the side that is receding from you).
- Draw a horizontal line to denote a floor or tabletop.

To draw a cylinder, draw two straight parallel lines the same length.

Connect the top with an oval and the bottom with half of an oval. Where is it in pictorial space?

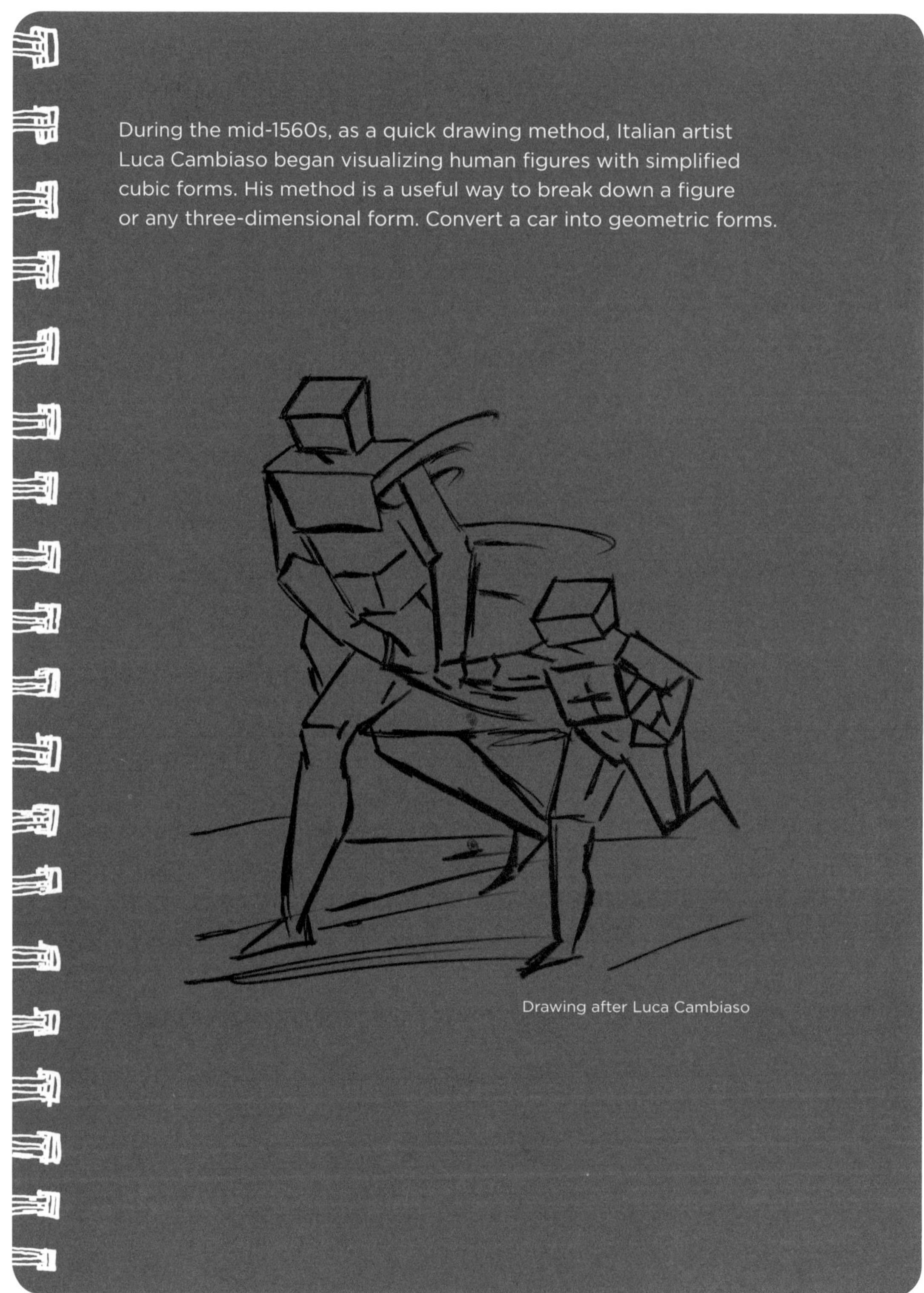

During the mid-1560s, as a quick drawing method, Italian artist Luca Cambiaso began visualizing human figures with simplified cubic forms. His method is a useful way to break down a figure or any three-dimensional form. Convert a car into geometric forms.

Drawing after Luca Cambiaso

How to Draw Graphic Space

Imagine this rectangle is a windowpane. At a point that is one-third of the page down from the top, draw a horizontal line across the rectangle.

Picture the top third as the sky and the bottom two-thirds as land. You just created a very simple open composition. The horizontal line is the horizon line.

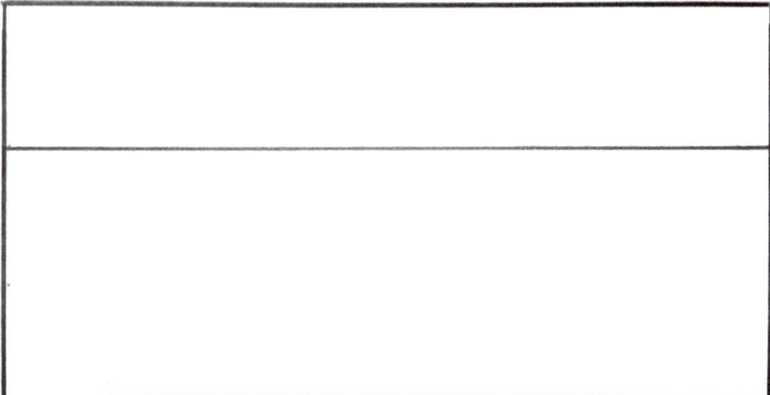

As soon as you draw a diagonal on a page, you begin to create the illusion of pictorial space. A titled plane can produce the illusion of a floor plane.

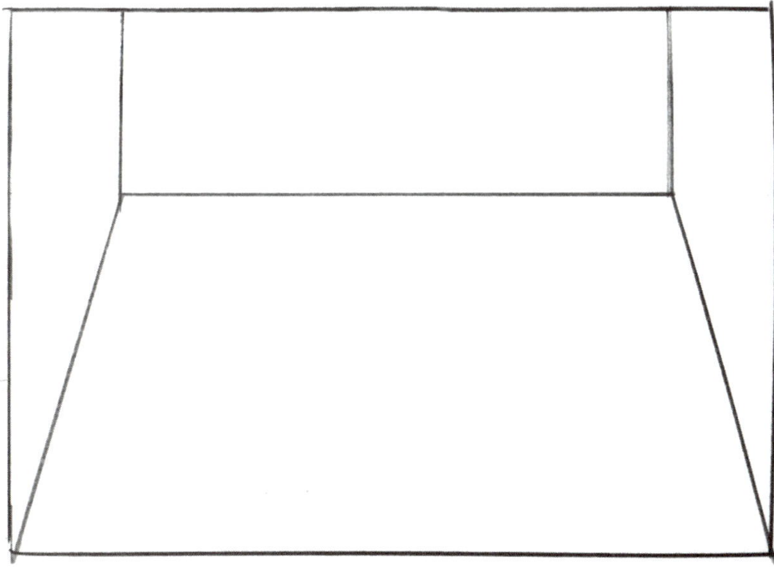

Imagine this rectangle is a room space, and you're looking straight ahead into the room at the back wall. At a point that is about one-third of the way from the bottom of the page, draw a long horizontal line. The ends of the line should not touch the edges of the rectangle, but stop short a couple of inches away on each side. Connect the drawn horizontal line to the sides of the page with a descending diagonal line at each end. You've created a tilted plane, which imitates a floor plane.

Now draw two vertical lines from each corner that connect the titled plane to the top edge of the rectangle. Now you have sketched a simple room space where the back wall appears to be farther away from you than the invisible front windowpane (picture plane).

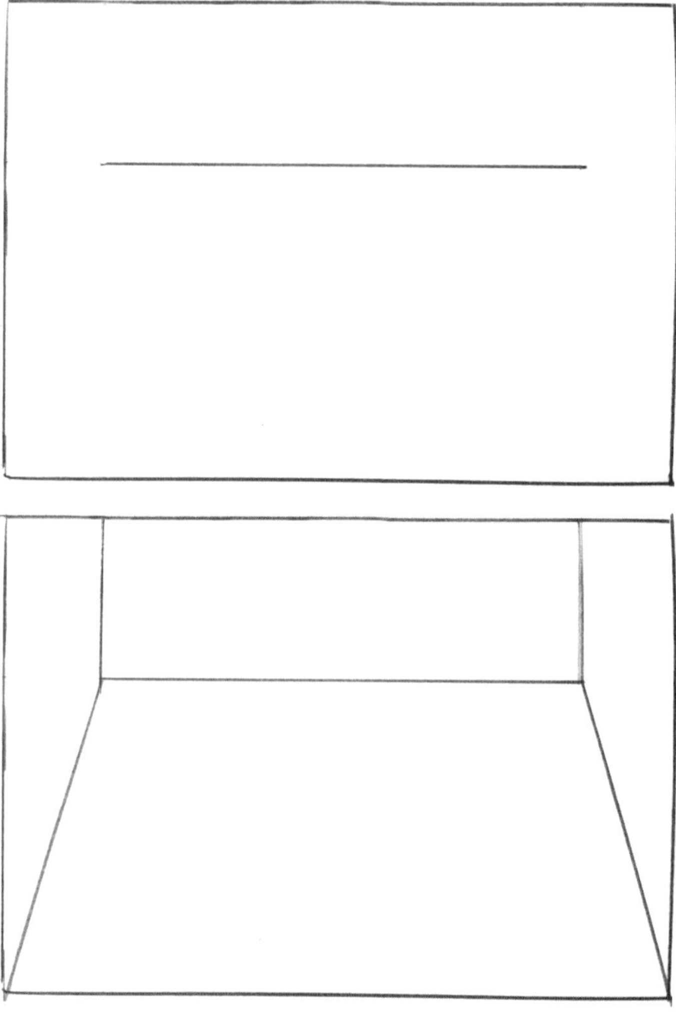

To draw a room in your home and its contents, begin by dividing the page into quadrants, which allows you to determine and record the position of objects in a real room space (or landscape, still life, or anything you care to draw from observation) onto a flat surface.

1. Divide your page into four equal quadrants with a horizontal and a vertical line.
   - The horizontal line will represent the place where the floor meets the wall. Anything in the room above that line will be drawn in the quadrants above the horizontal line.
   - The bottom of any object on the floor will be drawn below the horizontal line. If the objects on the floor rise above the line where the wall meets the floor, they will move into the upper quadrants.
2. Place a broomstick or any long straight object in the middle of the room space. The broomstick represents the vertical line that divides the page in half lengthwise. Or hold up a pencil in your line of vision. (Close one eye in order to determine how the space divides on either side of the pencil.)
3. Draw anything in the room that is to the right of the broomstick (or vertical line or pencil) in the right half quadrants.
4. Draw anything in the room space that is to the left of the broomstick (or vertical line or pencil) in the left-hand quadrants.

How to Draw Spatial Relationships

In Renaissance art, the illusion of spatial depth was created moving from foreground to background. The picture plane was thought of as a windowpane, with all forms receding back into pictorial space. During the Baroque era, artists broke through that front plane—the windowpane—creating the illusion of forms moving in front of as well as behind the picture plane. Think of a superhero comic in which the arm and fist of a figure punch through and penetrate the picture plane, as if it were actually moving into the viewer's space.

Earlier in this chapter, you learned how to draw forms. Now you are going to begin thinking compositionally. The following exercises will force you to think about space rather than rendering objects.

Principles of Composition

Just as drawing objects is governed by elemental forms, composing also has principles that, if employed, will improve your work.

In fine art and design, there are basic principles of composition—balance, emphasis, unity, and rhythm. These basic principles are absolutely interdependent.

- *Balance* is about stability and creating equilibrium.
- *Emphasis* is used to establish a point of focus in a composition and/or a visual hierarchy, which aids expression or communication.
- *Unity* is created in a composition when elements appear cohesive or have discernable visual relationships.
- *Rhythm* is a visual pulse and flow from one drawn element to another.

In fine art, you can break these rules for expressive reasons. In effective design and illustration, however, these rules are rarely if ever broken.

The following exercises will help you understand these principles and put them into practice.

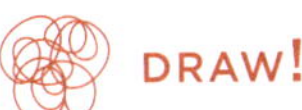

DRAW!

Front to Back: Set up a still life on a tabletop. The tabletop should be against a wall. Position yourself so that you can see the front edge of the table. Start by drawing the front edge (plane) of the table, the plane that is parallel to your page. Then look across the titled plane of the tabletop to draw the objects.

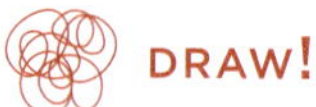

Back to Front: Set up a still life on a tabletop. The tabletop should be against a wall. Start by looking at the back wall. Draw what you see from that point of origin. If you compare the pictorial space in this drawing to the "Front to Back" prompt before this one, you'll notice that the objects in one composition look closer to you than in the other.

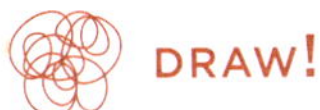

DRAW!

Symmetric Composition: Symmetry guarantees balance in a composition. This means there is a mirroring of equivalent elements, an equal distribution of visual weights, on either side of a central vertical axis. Compose a symmetrical composition. Whatever you draw on one side of this vertical axis, mirror it on the other side. Use nonrepresentational shapes, such as geometric or organic ones.

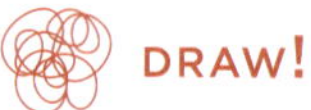

Asymmetric Composition: Asymmetry is an equal distribution of visual weights that is achieved through weight and counterweight, by balancing one element with the weight of a counterpointing element, *without mirroring* elements on either side of a central vertical axis. Compose an asymmetrical composition using nonrepresentational organic or geometric shapes.

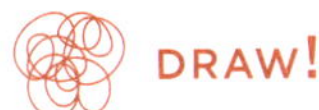

Visual Hierarchy: Draw three beach or soccer balls of varying sizes. Position them into a visual hierarchy. Using size, color, order, contrast, pattern, and/or position, direct the viewer's attention. Which one do you want the viewer to see first? Which one do you want the viewer to see second? Which one do you want the viewer to see third? Do the sizes and positions of the balls encourage the viewer to do what you want?

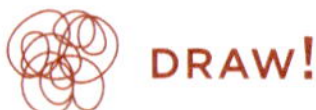

Focal Point as Point of Entry: Many drawings have a focal point, an image or component of the drawing that is emphasized, with other elements subordinate to it. Viewers seek a focal point, which allows them to visually enter the composition. Create emphasis—sketch one very big image, such as a dog or a biomorphic shape, which will act as the focal point. Any other marks or imagery you include should be subordinate to the point of focus.

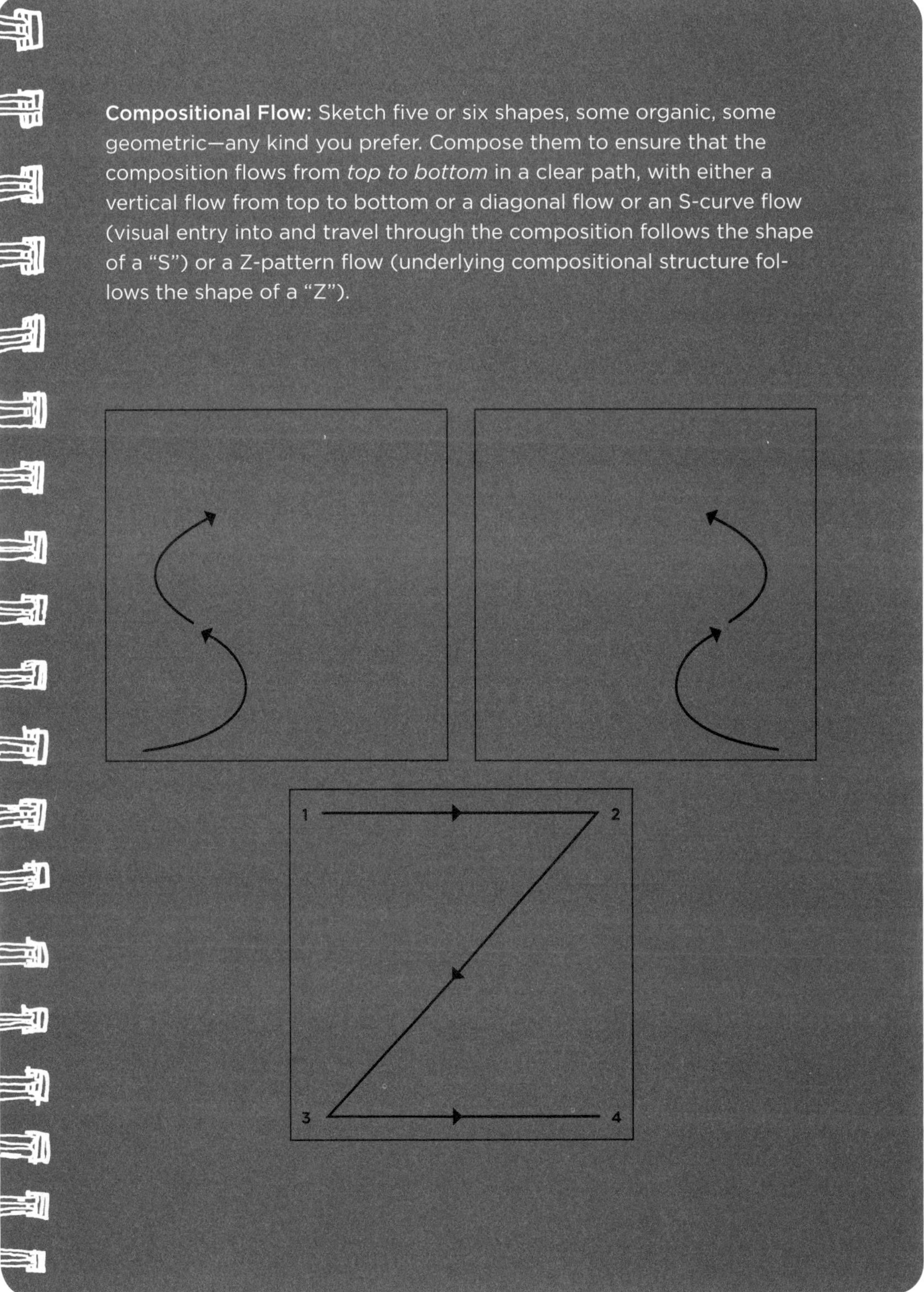

Compositional Flow: Sketch five or six shapes, some organic, some geometric—any kind you prefer. Compose them to ensure that the composition flows from *top to bottom* in a clear path, with either a vertical flow from top to bottom or a diagonal flow or an S-curve flow (visual entry into and travel through the composition follows the shape of a "S") or a Z-pattern flow (underlying compositional structure follows the shape of a "Z").

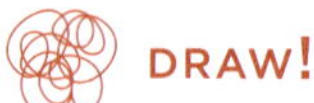

Directing the Viewer's Eye Scan: Sketch five or six shapes, some organic and some geometric—any kind you prefer. Compose them to ensure that the composition flows from *bottom to top* in a clear path, with either a vertical flow from bottom to top or a diagonal flow, or an S-curve flow or a Z-pattern flow.

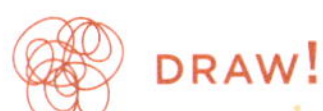

Emphasis through Direction: Use nine arrows (drawn any which way) to create a focal point on this page. Use the arrows to create emphasis by pointing to one specific location on the page.

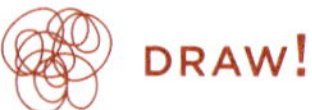

Emphasis through Contrast: Create a composition with a focal point (an object, a figure, a monster, etc.) created through contrast. The focal point should be much darker or brighter (if you are using color) than any other part of the composition.

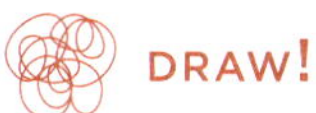

Rhythm and Flow: Dump out the contents of your pocket, handbag, or drawer. Arrange them on this page so that the position and direction of one object leads to the other. Once you are satisfied with the arrangement, move it off the page and re-create it from memory.

STEFAN G. BUCHER

{344LOVESYOU.COM}

"First make an ink blot, then add eyes, mouths, limbs...season to taste with pinstripes...Keep going until you've got yourself a monster."

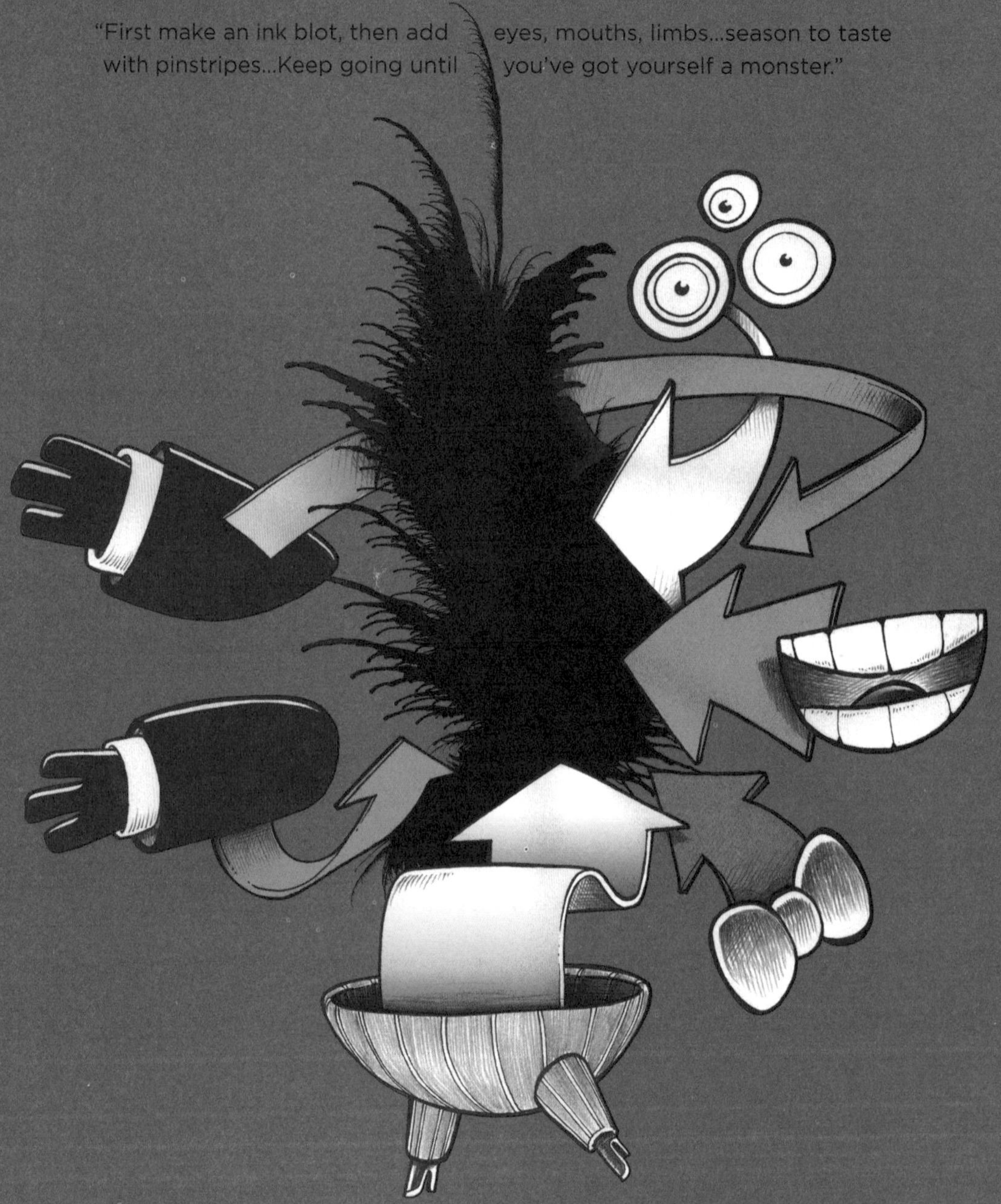

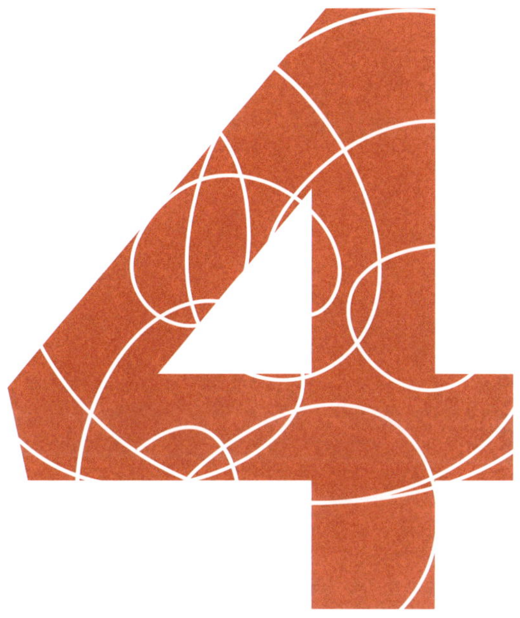

Just Draw with Lines!

Facing an empty page can be daunting, even for experienced visual artists. Artist James Romberger explains how one master cartoonist felt about the blank page.

"Mort Meskin [Golden Age comic book artist] was known to face an empty page with considerable trepidation, staring at it for hours in a total block. Eventually his studio mates figured out to go over and scribble a few random lines on his page, which he was then able to begin turning into a composition.

"According to Alex Toth [American comic book artist and animation designer], later in his career Meskin would shade the entire page with the flat side of a pencil lead, then begin to pick out white areas here and there with an eraser—in this way he was able to avoid the creative blocks that stymied his youth."

This chapter is full of ideas that will help you to get past any trepidation and just start drawing.

Start by Scribbling

Part 1. Find a piece of scrap paper. Or if you have a drawing tablet, use that. Start scribbling with abandon (try really hard if you're adverse to being messy or unrestricted). Be as unconstrained by preconceptions about making marks as you can. Scribble over scribbles, making some areas darker and denser than others. Fill the scrap of paper or digital page without concern about representing any person, place, or object.

Critique: Did you use your wrist? Was your arm resting on a table?

Do the scribbles drawn over scribbles look a bit like atmosphere? Did you create the illusion of spatial depth? Did you touch the edges of the page? Does the page look boundless?

Part 2. Find as big a piece of paper or substrate as you can, for example, a sheet of newsprint paper, an actual spread from a printed newspaper, a couple of paper towels, or the side of a big cardboard carton.

Put the substrate on the floor or on a table surface. Scribble. But this time, use your whole arm to make the marks. It's best if you stand while you do this. Use arm movements, not just wrist movements, to make marks.

As in Step 1, fill the entire surface without concern about representation or making anything other than marks.

Critique: Did using your arm feel differently than using your wrist to draw? Did the scribbles look different?

Line Palette: Assemble an assortment of pencils in varying degrees of hardness, for example, a 6B, 2B, and an H; a stick of charcoal; any kind of crayon; a fine-point marker; a brush plus ink or paint; an unconventional implement, such as a cotton swab, rosebud, or twig; ink or watered-down paint; and paper or this journal.

A line can have a specific *quality*—it can be thick or thin, solid or broken, continuous or noncontinuous (implied), changeless or varying, smooth or uneven, and so on. Using each drawing implement, sweep your hand across the page twice. The first swipe should be light and fast. The second swipe should be more controlled, pressing with a moderate amount of pressure.

Compare the marks. Can you match each mark with an emotion? An actual texture?

Draw a light, long line. Then draw a scratchy long line.

Determine several types of lines that you can draw with the *same* pencil; for example, a light, delicate line; an uneven line; a rough line; a smudged or messy line; a dark, thicker line; a staggered line; and so on.

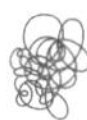

Use a tool to its full potential but never force a tool to make a mark it wasn't meant to produce. Use a drawing implement for its innate quality. If you want a dark line, for instance, use a soft pencil or another appropriate tool. (Some artists and designers deliberately force a tool to make unnatural marks, but they have some expressive intention in mind.)

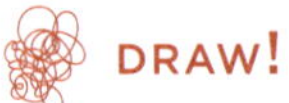

DRAW!

Create a palette of lines (an assorted range) using more than one drawing tool. For example, use an H pencil and a Conté crayon.

Look out of a window. Use your palette of lines to draw what you see, being mindful of how each line quality contributes to the overall emotional tone or communication.

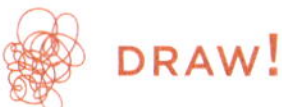

Continuous Contour: Imagine a leaf or daisy. Or find a leaf or flower as a visual reference. Using an unbroken line, draw the outer shape of the leaf or flower so that it fills the entire page. Don't worry about drawing details but do carefully examine the outer shape of the object, drawing with as much specificity to the shape as possible. Go as near to the edges of the page as possible. Once you start drawing, keep your pencil moving on the page. Don't lift your hand to stop and start. (Search online to see American artist Ellsworth Kelly's plant drawings.)

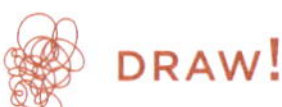

Continuous Line: The best tool for this project is a soft pencil, fine line marker, digital pen, or your finger on a touchscreen. Your subject matter will be a room space, still life, figure in space, or yourself.

Once you start drawing a line, your drawing tool maintains contact with the page, producing a continuous (unbroken) line.

Think of this exercise as if you were taking a line for a walk through graphic space. Use the line to describe whatever you are looking at, if you have a life reference. You can use a continuous line to draw from your imagination, as well. To describe enclosed shapes, simply overlap the line. The objects and spaces will appear to look transparent.

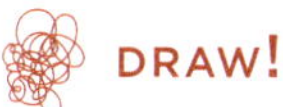

DRAW!

Blind Contour: Pretend you are drawing a big circle on this page, a circle that almost touches the boundaries of the page, *without* looking at the page.

Now, actually draw the contour of an object or form that has an interesting silhouette, such as a crab or shoe, but do not look at the page—look only at the subject matter. Make it as big as possible, feeling for the boundaries of the page as you draw. Don't be concerned with the end result as much as with experiencing this *blind contour* process.

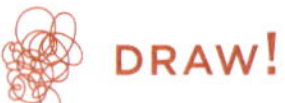

Quick Contour: Ask a friend to pose for you. Use a single line to record the contour of the figure. The goal is to quickly record a general gesture. Study the figure for its general shape, drawing as rapidly as possible (about 15 to 60 seconds). Repeat this several times. Repeat it again, allotting up to two minutes. You may need more paper. (If you don't have a friend around, use an object or animal as reference for these rapid sketches.)

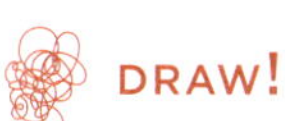

DRAW!

Cross Contour: Look at a spherical object or form, such as a coffee mug, a pear, or your hand. Draw the form's outline and add cross-contour lines (parallel lines that curve to describe the form's rounded volume).

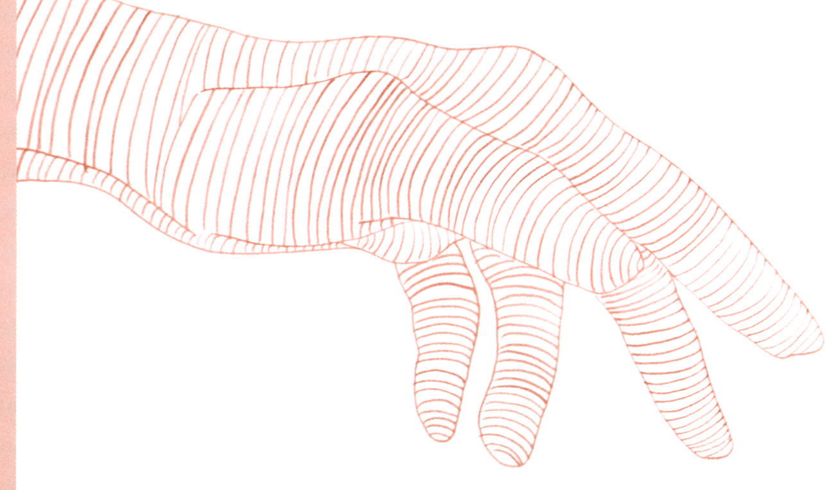

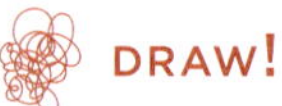

Flowing Line: Start drawing a line at the top-left corner of the page. Allow yourself to draw whatever comes to mind—a spiral, a vine, a flower, a figure, or a car. Use a flowing, lyrical line to create the form. (Search online to see drawings by French artist Henri Matisse.)

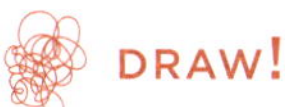

Distressed Line: Using lines made with charcoal or a very soft pencil, draw something that upsets you. Smudge and scrape the lines.

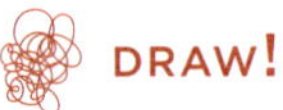

Implied Line: Draw a car using broken lines that describe enough for the viewer to understand the shape without closing or completing the lines.

Organizational Lines: Using a soft pencil, draw a still life, interior space, or cityscape. Based on careful observations of all major vertical and horizontal emphases within the subject matter, begin by drawing horizonal and vertical lines that will serve to build the composition, to create structural axes as well as describe forms.

Organizational lines display and emphasize the structural axes of a composition and link forms in space. Simultaneously, the lines organize the pictorial space, create the illusion of spacial depth through overlapping, and define objects.

After establishing the relative heights of forms using horizontal and vertical lines, extend those lines further beyond the forms they describe into adjacent forms, as if the objects were transparent. The lines also extend into the surrounding pictorial space, as if the lines were a beam searching the pictorial space. For example, if you're drawing a chair in a room space, the lines you draw to define the chair also act to partially define the pictorial space of the room, the wall and floor, and any objects next to or overlapping the chair.

You can use sighting—holding up your pencil in front of you and using it as a measuring tool to compare relative heights and widths of objects in your subject matter—to determine the relative heights, widths, and angles.

Jonathan KYLE Farmer, ma(rca)

{ASSOCIATE PROFESSOR OF FASHION,
PARSONS THE NEW SCHOOL FOR DESIGN}

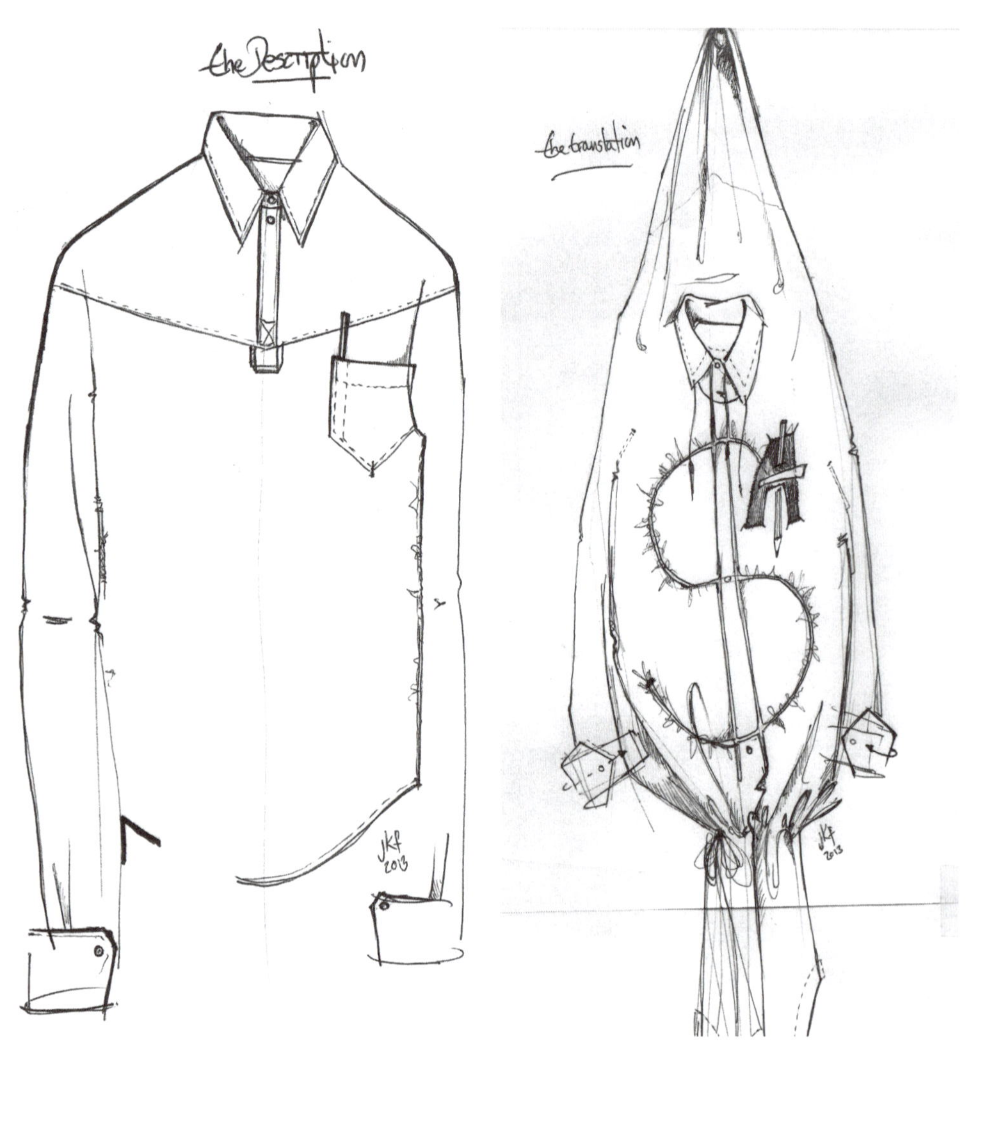

FASHION AND TRANSLATION: DESCRIBE IT, DRAW IT. TRANSLATE IT, DRAW IT.

The description:
WHAT IS SH.I.RT?

It is a white button-up shirt with the placket set for a male wearer.

The collar is medium spread with a matching thread topstitch.

The buttons are made of mother-of-pearl.

The side seams are flat-felled and cause a slight puckering in the seams from the tight stitches being laundered but not ironed.

There is a breast pocket on the left-hand side. It is the traditional shape, a square with a V-shape at the bottom.

In addition to the horizontal topstitch about 1.25 inches from the top of the pocket, it is also topstitched into two sections.

The topstitch is about an inch from the center side of the pocket, giving it a small section that a pen or pencil would easily slip into.

The sleeve is a one-piece sleeve with a barrel cuff.

The cuff has a single button and an angled cutout on the overlap.

The hem of the shirt is long enough to stay inside the pants when tucked in and has a slight curve on the sides.

The yoke of the shirt has no topstitch and there is a fabric-hanging loop centered at the back base of the yoke.

DRAW IT:

A TRANSLATION:
English → Greek → German → Arabic → Chinese → English

His is a button on a white shirt placket male users.

Collar is a match for the string before the needle deployment.

Mother-of-pearl buttons.

Side of the sewing at seams and a slight wrinkle layers close to the money-laundering networks, but not normal.

There is a pocket on the left.

This is the traditional form of the letter box at the end of the horizontal seam in addition to the constraints 1.25 inches from the top of the pocket all the parts.

At the top about an inch from center to his side pocket a small part, pen, or pencil can be easily changed.

Cover part of the sleeve and the sleeve of the barrel.

Rotator cuff contains a button and a corner piece of the paint. In the hem of the shirt long enough to stay in his pants, when they came to a slight curve on the side.

Yoke shirt sewing machines and fabric with the highest hanging ring in the middle of the rear base of the yoke."

DRAW IT:

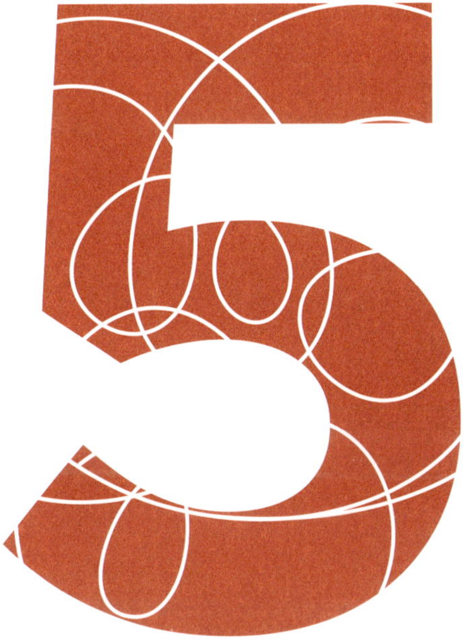

Shape, Plane, Volume, and Perspective

What do the depiction of a flying superhero, a tree, a building, and cones and cylinders floating in graphic space all have in common? Drawing them means you have to create the illusion of volume. To draw subjects you observe or invent—ranging from precisely rendered figures to geometric nonobjective forms—you need to learn how to create and manipulate shapes, planes, and volume. And you need to have a basic grasp of perspective.

Shape

If you prefer the silhouette of one car over another, you are responding to shape. A *shape* is the general outline of an object, figure, or form. Shapes are flat, without volume, like a triangle that you draw on paper. You can create them with line, value, texture, or color.

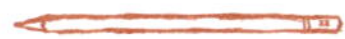

A *representational* shape resembles something in nature or our environment like the shape of a butterfly. An *abstract* shape visualizes a simple or complex alteration of natural appearance. A *nonobjective* shape is purely invented; it does not literally represent a person, place, or thing.

Representational, abstract, and nonobjective shapes can be geometric, organic, or irregular.

- A *geometric* (rigid) shape is characterized by straight edges, precise curves, or measurable angles, such as a square, triangle, or trapezoid.
- An *organic*, curvilinear, free form, or biomorphic shape is characterized by curves or flowing edges, which can be deliberate or accidental.
- An *irregular* shape is a combination of straight and curved lines.

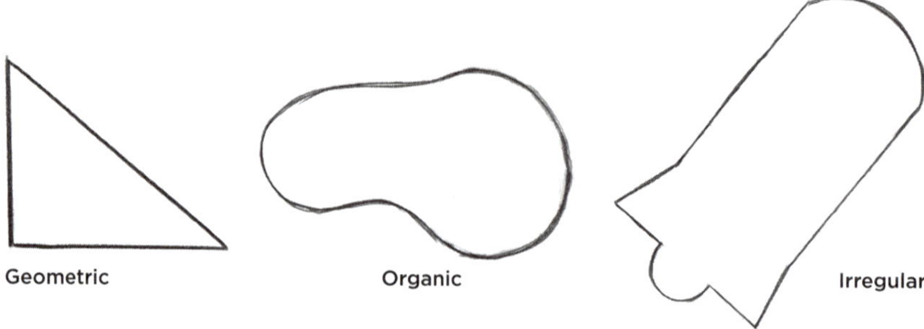

Plane and Volume

A *plane* is a two-dimensional surface. It has a shape, like this page. Shapes can function as planes to build volume.

To draw a cube, for example, you need to create the illusion of a volume on a flat page or screen. An actual cube has six planes. However, if you were to draw a cube from observation, you would not see all of its surfaces simultaneously. (If your goal is something other than realism, certainly, you could draw all six for an expressive purpose.) If you were perfectly eye level with one side of a cube, it would look like a square. If your eye level were slightly above a cube, you would see it has volume because you'd see its top plane.

Any object, creature, person, or environmental structure (natural or constructed) has mass or volume. All of these can be represented on a flat surface. In life and in three-dimensional visual arts, such as sculpture, there is mass and void. In two-dimensional visual arts, there is positive and negative form or figure and ground.

You can transform a shape into a volumetric form as well as create the illusion of masses and voids on a flat surface through a variety of means—using line, value, perspective, color, or modeling with tone (the change from light to dark across a surface to create the illusion of volume, which you will explore further in Chapter 6).

The Picture Plane

The *picture plane* is the blank, flat, two-dimensional surface of a page, like a pane of glass in a window. You can keep the picture plane flat by using flat shapes or lines that emphasize its characteristic flatness. Or you can create the illusion of depth by manipulating the picture plane. Any drawn mark you make on the surface affects the appearance and graphic position of the picture plane.

In Renaissance art, the picture plane was regarded as a picture window, just like a real glass window, where the illusion of depth moves behind the picture plane. During the Baroque period, artists regarded the picture plane as more malleable, creating the illusion of forms moving in front of the picture plane, penetrating it. This is similar to the notion of graphic space in comic books, where a thrown punch looks like it's coming out into your space.

You also can manipulate graphic space to create the illusion of spatial planes. As explained in the first chapter of this book, there are three key planes with others in between: the foreground, middle ground, and background.

You can draw and arrange those spatial planes so that they seem to recede back behind the picture plane. Or you can create pictorial space that appears to move both in front of and behind the picture plane. The illusion of depth can be shallow or deep. You can manipulate spatial planes or keep the page flat looking.

You can create a logical arrangement of spatial planes, where some are obviously closer to the viewer than others. Or you can create equivocal (ambiguous spatial relationships) or even logic-defying graphic or pictorial space. Imagery can be representational, abstract, or nonobjective.

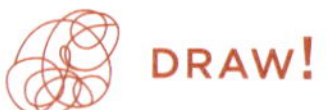

Place your nondrawing hand with fingers spread wide on this page, positioning your hand so that you create interesting shape relationships between it and the page's boundaries. (Your hand is the positive shape, and the shapes between your hand and the page are negative shapes.) Add small geometric and organic shapes in the negative spaces.

Finally, divide the big hand shape into smaller geometric and organic shapes.

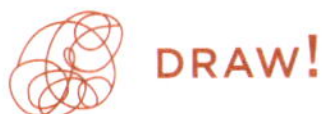

DRAW!

Find a toy or interestingly shaped object. Draw the contour of the object to fill the space, creating interesting negative shapes with the page's edges.

Next, fill in the negative shapes with color and/or visual texture.

Finally, color in the positive shape or fill with tone or texture.

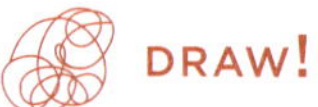

Find an object, such a scissors or leaf—something with an interesting silhouette—or imagine the shape of a bird or hair dryer. If you have black paper, cut the object's shape out of the paper (don't draw it first), making it big enough to create an interesting composition on this page. Adhere it. Or create the silhouette with black ink, acrylic paint, or black crayon. Write random or chosen words in the negative spaces.

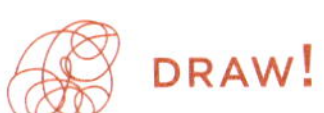

Merge two shapes. For example, create a composite shape of a donkey and an elephant, a glove and a rabbit, or a crescent and a hammer.

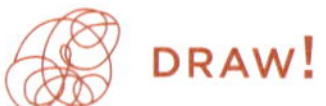

DRAW!

Position a chair in front of you so that you can see its legs touching the floor.

Draw and compose the chair on this page so that the full length of the chair, from the top of the back to the tip of the legs, fills the vertical length of the page. Include a floor line.

Now you'll approach this exercise differently (use a new sheet of paper). Again, position a chair in front of you so that you can see its legs touching the floor.

Draw and compose the chair on the page so that its full length, from the top of the back to the tip of the legs, fills the vertical length of the page. But this time, draw only the negative shapes the chair makes with the space. (You'll be tempted to draw the chair itself, but resist.)

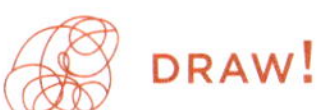

DRAW!

Sketch a leafy plant by drawing only the shapes between the leaves and stems, *not* the forms (leaves, stems, etc.) themselves. Do this exercise many times using different subject matter. *Look for the negative shape relationships in everything you see.*

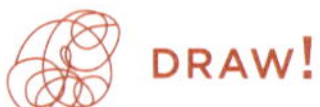

"Observe a tree in winter bare of leaves and re-create it on paper by drawing the negative spaces rather than the positive."
—April D. Allen, Ph.D., Assistant Professor, Interior Design, Michigan State University

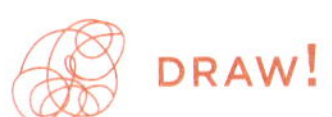

DRAW!

Value Scale: This technical exercise will help you learn to create a range of grays.

1. Collect or print out a variety of grays as well as a black and a white value. Or mix the grays from nontoxic black and white acrylic paint, or instead of all of the above, use drawing software.
2. Lay out the samples to create an even ten-step gradation scale of grays ranging from white to black.
3. Cut all ten samples into the same geometric shape.
4. Arrange the shapes into a gradation scale, from white to black.
5. Create a duplicate gray scale by hand, using a drawing tool and technique of preference (hatching, solid tone, etc.).

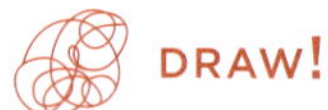

Draw four cubes. Embellish these forms with shading (tones created by hatched pencil lines or solid sweeps of charcoal or crayon) to create the illusion of three dimensions. On each of the cubes, use a different technique or element—for example, hatching, solid tone, texture, or color.

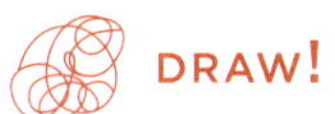

Draw a tree on the left-hand side of this page. The height of the tree should run the vertical length of the page, with the bottom of the tree almost cut off at the bottom of the page. Draw a horizon line behind the tree, a line to indicate where the sky meets the ground.

Where does the tree appear to be in the pictorial space?

Next, draw another tree behind the first tree. (The bottom of the second tree should be higher up from the bottom of the page than the bottom of the first tree.) The overlapping trees should create the illusion of spatial depth.

Perspective

Perspective is a schematic technique used to depict spatial relationships and the illusion of volume on a flat surface. It is based on the idea that diagonals moving toward a point on the horizon, called the *vanishing point,* will converge. This imitates the recession of space into the distance and creates the illusion of spatial depth (think railroad tracks).

If you want to draw a cityscape (a view of a city), you have to interpret the three-dimensional forms you see in the environment and then translate them for a two-dimensional drawing. You can do this by eyeballing or by using perspective. Either way, first you have to determine your eye level, which is represented by a horizontal line called the *horizon line.* The horizon line represents your eye level and the viewer's eye level, and it usually indicates where land or water converges with the sky.

Your point of view is also the viewer's point of view. It can be straight ahead, above (a bird's-eye view) or below (a bug's-eye view). If you were standing at the foot of a staircase and were to draw a figure standing at the top of stairs, you would have a bug's-eye view. If you were standing at the top of the stairs and were to draw a figure at the foot of the staircase, you would have a bird's-eye view. If you were to draw a figure standing on the floor in front of you, your point of view would be straight ahead.

Here are ways that you can create the illusion of spatial depth through how you draw.

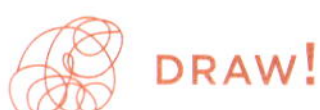

Railroad Tracks: Draw a horizon line. In the middle of the horizon line, draw a dot, which will represent the vanishing point. Draw one diagonal from each bottom corner of the page to connect to the vanishing point. Draw railroad tracks in between the diagonal lines. Add whatever else you like.

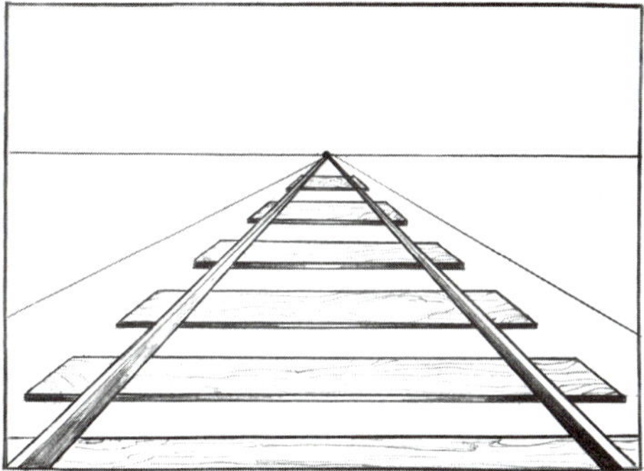

One-point Perspective: Draw a horizon line.

1. In the middle of the horizon line, draw a dot, which will represent the vanishing point. Anything you draw below the horizon line sits on the ground. Anything you draw above the horizon line moves into the sky.
2. Draw an X across the page with the center of the X at the vanishing point.
3. Draw buildings or trees on the left- and right-hand sides of the page; the vertical lines of the buildings or trees should parallel the vertical sides of the page. The top and bottom of the buildings should follow the diagonal paths created by the X.

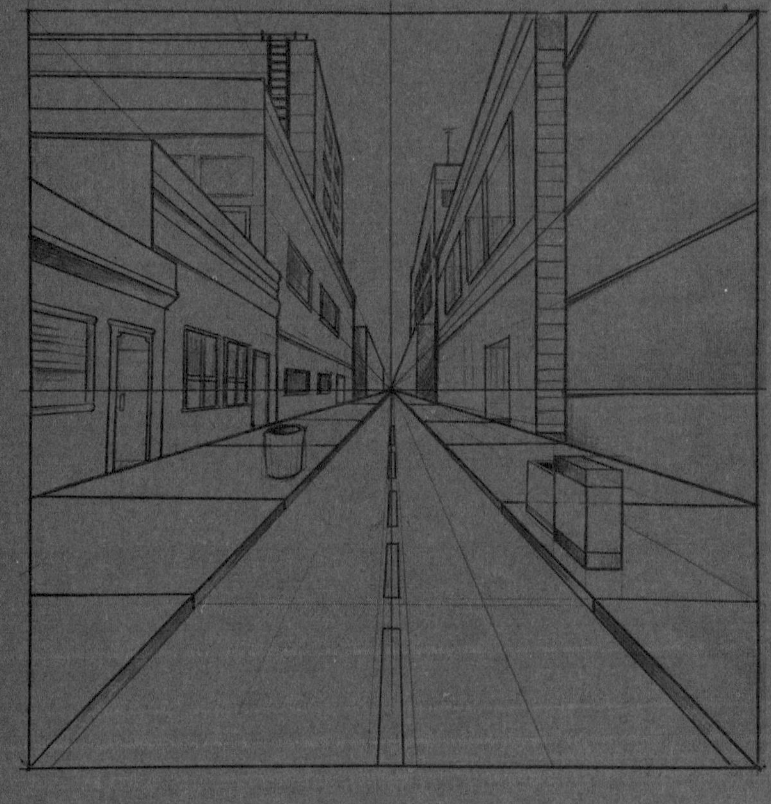

Two-point Perspective: Draw (or rule) a horizon line.

1. At each end of the horizon line, draw a dot to represent two vanishing points.
2. Draw a vertical line in the center of the horizon line. The vertical line represents the edge of a building, where two sides of the building converge.
3. Using a straightedge, rule diagonal lines from each vanishing point to the top and bottom of the center vertical line.
4. About half-way between the center and each edge of the page, rule two vertical lines to complete the building.

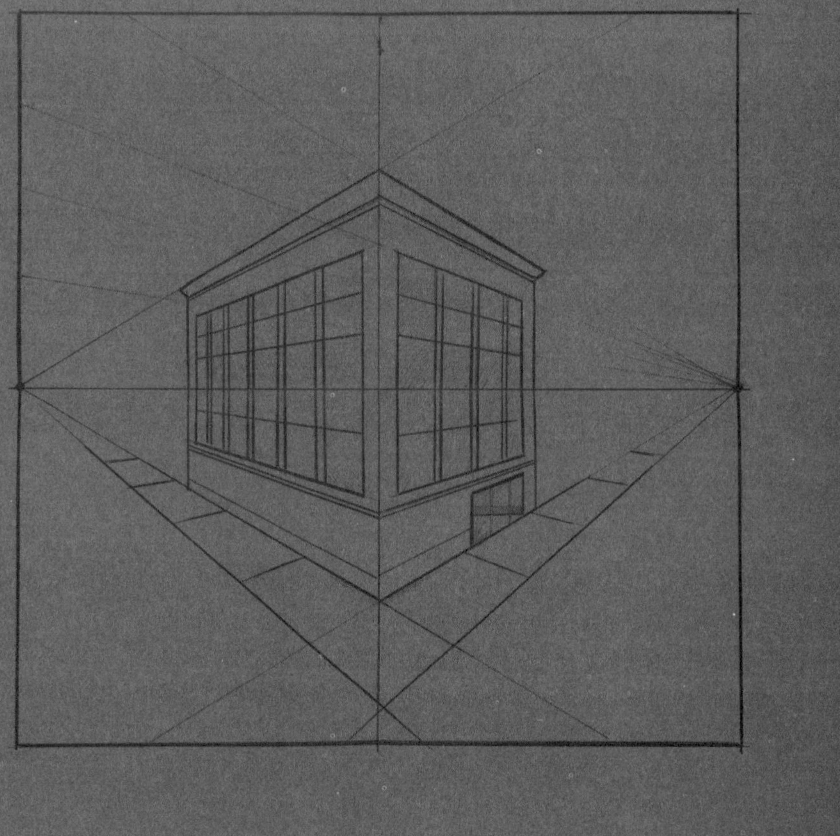

Mark Romanoski

{ARTIST, WWW.MARK-ROMANOSKI.COM}

"Do not try to be perfect when you draw—it's too intimidating. Every day, just try to draw better than you did the day before."

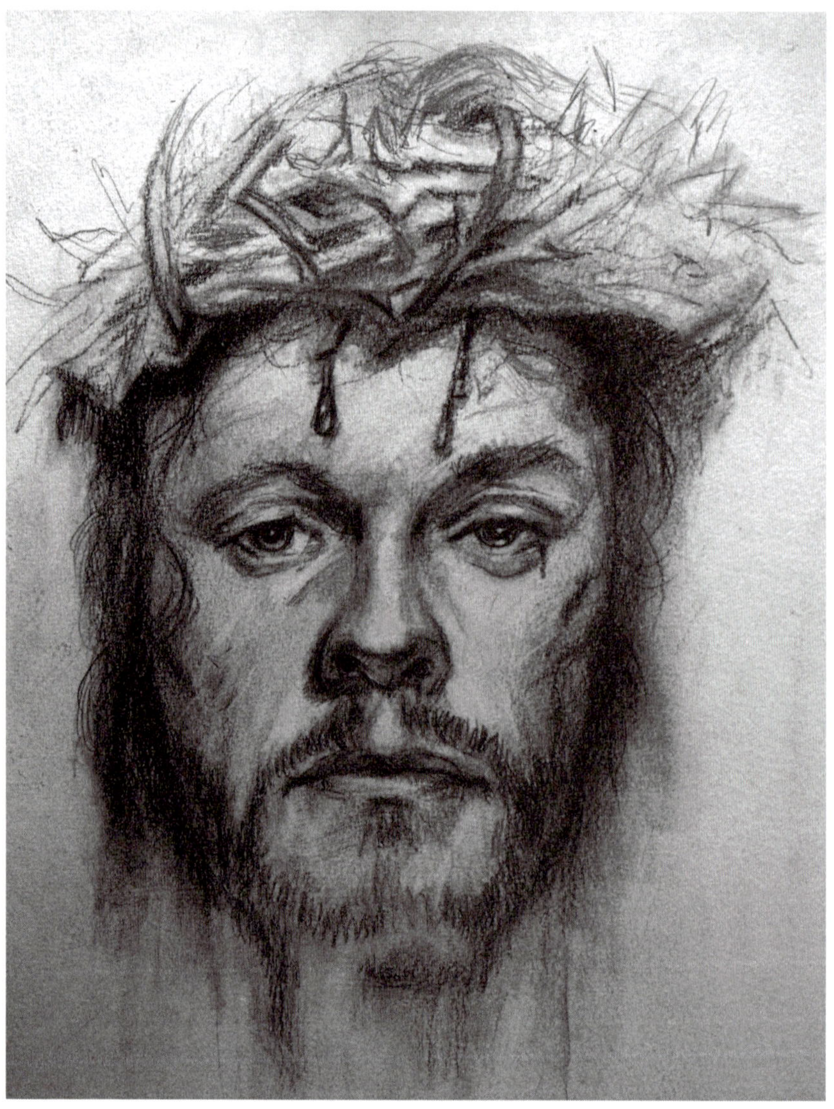

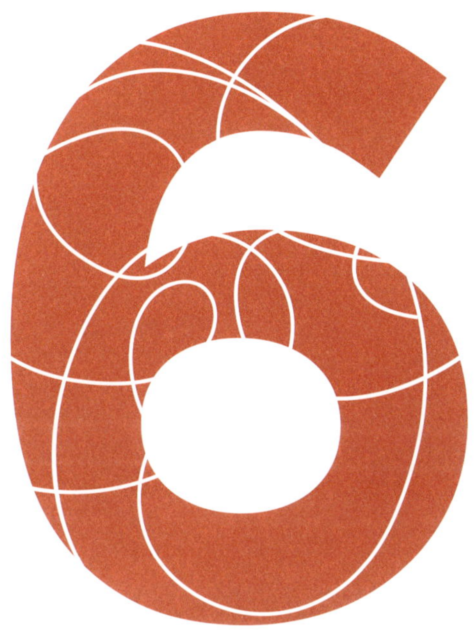

Still Life and Landscape

People appreciate still life and revel in landscape subjects. Designer Henry Sene Yee offers this insight into why people enjoy them so much. He says that still life and landscape are "evidence of constant and change in our constantly moving lives."

"Still life is unchanging and controlled (except for natural light). Landscape is ever changing, moment to moment in atmosphere/weather/light. In a moment the image no longer exists," adds animator Liz Blazer. Both subjects afford artists the chance to investigate how they see and record what they see.

Those subjects are perfect stepping stones in an artist's education—artists can use them to improve observational skills, advises designer Ria Venturina, and to learn to differentiate between looking and active seeing.

Still Life

During the sixteenth century in Northern Europe, Italy, and Spain, artists depicted still-life subjects—plants, animals, and man-made objects. Like scientists of the time, artists turned to direct observation to fathom the world.

Still life remains very popular among artists, from old masters such as French artist Paul Cézanne, Italian artist Giorgio Morandi, and American artist Georgia O'Keefe to contemporary artists. It is accessible, can be symbolic, makes the fleeting permanent, and can be the most mundane or exotic subject matter.

Still-life subjects can be almost anything: a breakfast; a tabletop scene; *vanitas* (objects that refer to the transience of life); a game; flowers and insects; common objects as well as luxurious ones. They can be mundane, be meaningful to the artist, or be symbolic to a specific audience.

Landscape

Landscapes are a favorite subject matter for artists and audiences. Before photography and film, landscapes were objects of contemplation, a world of escape answering a sense of longing.

This broad category also includes any kind of outdoor environment, such as seascape, mountainscape, or cityscape (a view of a city or suburban environment). Any kind of creature can inhabit your landscape. Although some artists think of interior spaces as much different subjects than landscapes because of their intimacy, we'll include them here as accessible drawing subjects.

Landscapes provide a sense of place. For most landscapes, you don't need to know any special story or iconography (symbols in works of art); it is what it is—everyone can relate to what you draw. Artists use a multitude of expressive marks and styles to draw landscapes—from flowing continuous lines to coarse slug-like marks.

Designer Rose Gonnella comments, "Landscape is an endless supply of line, shape, and form of a most beautiful variety at that. For me, it is all about the bounty of organic form. Man can never create the awesome variety that is nature. Nature supplies infinite subject matter for human endeavors in art and design."

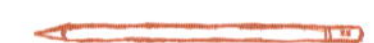

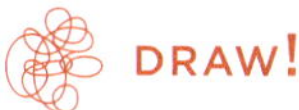

Position some fruits and a bowl on a tabletop. Overlap them. Draw the objects as close to their actual size as you can on this page.

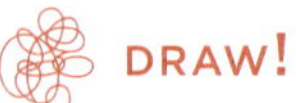

Position some fruits and a bowl on a tabletop. Overlap them. Draw the objects *smaller* than their actual size on this page. (This drawing should look different than the one you executed on the previous page.)

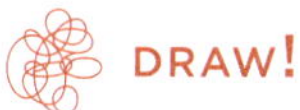

Arrange several objects on a tabletop (for example, two bowls, a cup, fruit, books, or anything that's available). Overlap the objects. Position them to span a good amount of the tabletop surface. Add cloth to the still life arrangement, if available.

Start drawing from the left-hand side of the still life and proceed moving toward the right-hand side, across the still life and page. Concern yourself with the transitions between objects. (Pretend the interstices have invisible connections between forms.) Don't worry about details but only about the shape relationships between objects.

Don't refer back to the left-hand side as you draw. Don't go back to make adjustments.

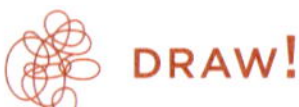

Use the same still-life arrangement as on the previous page.

Start your drawing at any point on the page. Think about where the viewer should enter the pictorial space. Consider where each object is in relation to the objects next to it. Focus on the relative heights and widths and the spaces between objects, again pretending the interstices have invisible connections between forms.

Chiaroscuro is an Italian art term that refers to the use of contrasting light and dark in a drawing or painting.

Materials: white drawing paper; soft vine charcoal; kneaded eraser; nontoxic, workable fixative.

Subject matter: Still-life objects. Suggestion: If you don't have any objects available, you can cover tea boxes and cereal boxes with white paper.

Setup: On a tabletop, arrange a still life comprised of objects of your choice. Illuminate the still life with a direct light (window light or lamp) from either the left or right side, not top or bottom. Do not use diffused light. You need extreme light and dark contrasts, such as the light and dark contrast found in works by Italian artist Caravaggio, Dutch artist Rembrandt van Rijn, or French artist Georges de La Tour. (Visit online to see the works by Caravaggio, Rembrandt, and de La Tour.)

Procedure (be forewarned—this is a messy technique):

1. Cover the entire paper with an even coat of charcoal. The charcoal on the paper represents the dark.
2. You will be drawing with the eraser to create the light, unlike most drawing techniques where you draw in the shadows. Observing the extreme light falling on the objects, tabletop, and background, make judgments about which areas you will erase.
3. Simply erase the broadest areas that represent the light. Don't worry about details.
4. Erased areas should create a logical flow of light throughout the entire composition.
5. You can easily make corrections by re-covering areas with charcoal. You can go back and forth with the eraser and charcoal.
6. Go back in with the charcoal to accent cast shadows and darker areas.
7. Spray the finished drawing with nontoxic fixative in a well-ventilated room or outside.

In this exercise, you will be creating a tonal drawing, working from a middle ground tone.

Materials: Medium-toned (tan or gray) paper for charcoal or chalk drawings; white and black chalk or Conté crayon; a graphite pencil; vine or compressed charcoal; nontoxic fixative.

Setup: Arrange a still life lighted from one side or find an old master painting from which to draw, such as a work by the seventeenth-century Dutch painter Johannes Vermeer. (It's advisable to draw from an old master painting rather than an old master drawing. That way you're interpreting rather than copying.)

In preparation:

1. You can purchase the paper you need for this exercise, such as Toned Sketch Paper from Strathmore. Some people prefer to tone paper themselves using paint, ink, cold tea, or cold coffee to create an overall tan, even tone. If you tone white paper, allow time for drying, and weight down the paper to avoid curling.
2. Some people like using a viewfinder as a drawing aid. A viewfinder is a cardboard or plastic rectangular frame with a rectangular window opening, meant to frame the scene or subject matter. The edges of the viewfinder correspond to the edges of the paper, allowing you to see how the forms would be positioned in a composition. To make a viewfinder from cardboard just cut out a rectangular hole, which will be the viewfinder window. If you are using 9x12-inch paper to draw on, the window should be in proportion, that is, 3x4 inches.
3. If you are drawing from an old master, you may want to make a grid on transparent film, which you can place over the reproduction to see where elements would fall in the composition. You can do without graphic aids and make all judgments by eye.

Procedure:

1. Begin by making judgments about where objects will be positioned in the composition.
2. You will create a tonal sketch(es) making dark and light marks and working from a middle ground.
3. Use the white drawing tool to represent the light. Draw all the areas where the light hits the forms.
4. Use the black drawing tool to create shadows or the darkest areas.
5. All other planes will be represented by the medium tone of the paper, which will serve as the compositional unifier and tonal backbone of the drawing. The viewer will be able to read the light across the composition, moving from one form to the next. The black areas will aid in creating volume by acting as the most recessive planes, shadowed areas, and cast shadows.
6. When you are finished, spray the drawing with nontoxic fixative in a well-ventilated room or outdoor space.

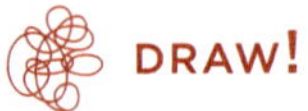

DRAW!

When a landscape is held in a vertical orientation, you can conceive the pictorial space as divisions or zones of sky and land; as heaven, earth, and the underworld; or as any kind of vertical integration you desire.

Draw a landscape in a vertical orientation with deliberate horizontal divisions or zones.

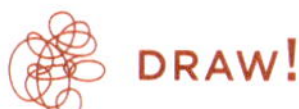

Draw a landscape in a vertical orientation, where there is a deliberate movement up the pictorial space or down the pictorial space.

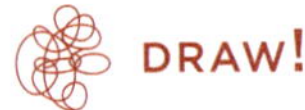

When a landscape is held in a horizontal orientation, you can create an illusion of movement across the horizontal format—for example, a procession, a parade, horses galloping across the land, and so on. (Visit metmuseum.org to see French artist Rosa Bonheur's *The Horse Fair*.)

Draw a landscape with the illusion of movement horizontally across the page.

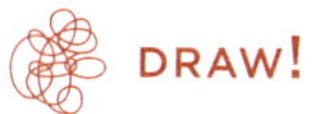

To create asymmetrical compositions, some artists employ the Rule of Thirds (see Chapter 1). Use the Rule of Thirds to draw a landscape or cityscape.

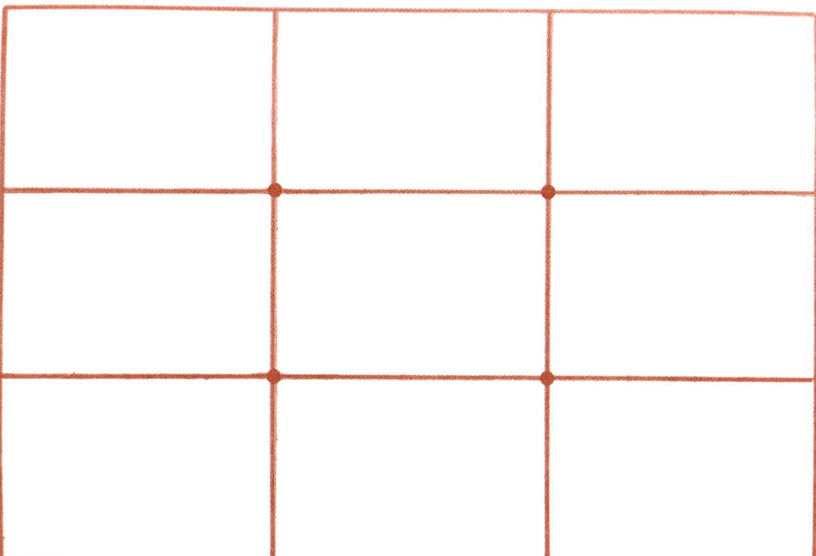

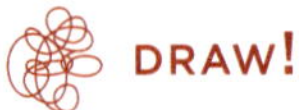

In Western representational art, the viewer often enters the composition across the ground plane. This can happen at the left-hand edge, the center, or the right-hand edge. The path of the viewer's eyes travel along the ground plane, then is further directed by the compositional arrangement to a focal point, then on to a secondary focal point, and so on.

Sketch a landscape with a point of entry across the ground plane. The path should be an "S" curve.

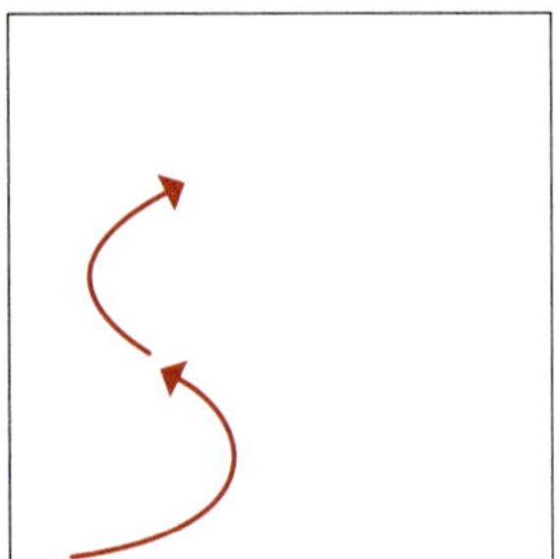

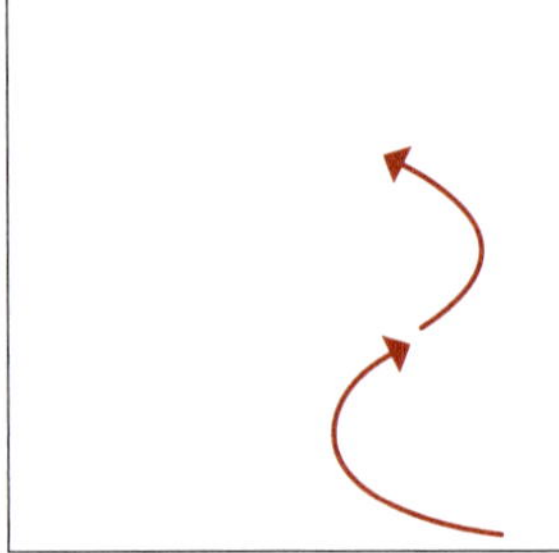

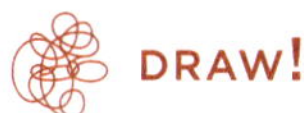

Compose an asymmetric drawing with a large form, such as a tree or building, in the foreground acting as an entry point into the composition.

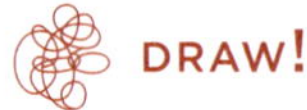

"Draw 20 overlapping pyramids, then fill different shapes with different colors."

—Ellen Yi-Luen Do, Professor of Industrial Design and Interactive Computing, College of Architecture and College of Computing, Georgia Institute of Technology

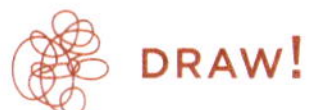

Sketch an interior or cityscape with a point of entry across the ground plane. Guide the path of the viewer's eyes into your composition in a "Z" pattern.

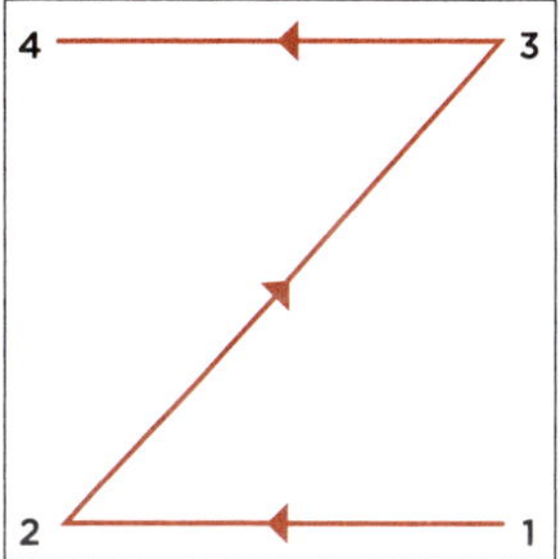

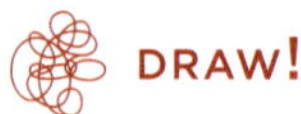

Sketch a landscape, interior, or cityscape with a point of entry created by a dominate diagonal movement aimed at the focal point, for example, a long diagonal branch from a cropped tree in the foreground aimed at a focal point.

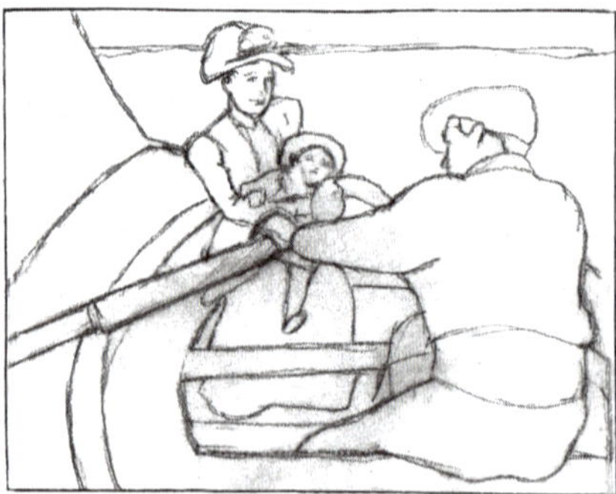

Drawing after a Mary Cassatt

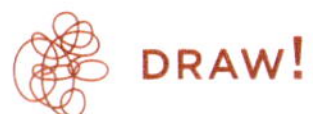

DRAW!

Sketch a landscape, interior, or cityscape with a point of entry created by a big shape or form that flows rhythmically to other smaller forms.

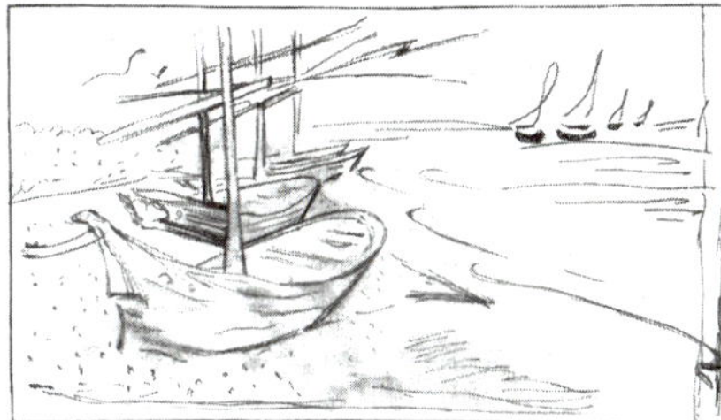

Drawing after a Vincent van Gogh

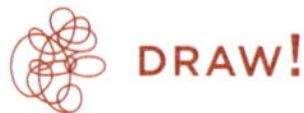

DRAW!

Sketch a landscape with a long road coming from the bottom left or right edge as the point of entry into your composition. (To see another example, search *Rain, Steam, and Speed—the Great Western Railway,* by J.M.W. Turner, in the National Gallery, London.)

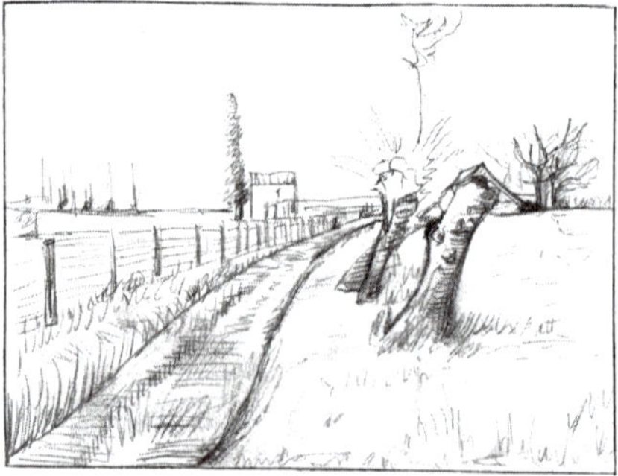

Drawing after a Vincent van Gogh

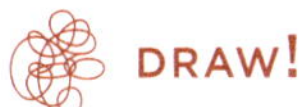

DRAW!

Create the illusion of atmosphere in a landscape drawing. Use vine charcoal or a soft pencil to modulate tones. Things in the foreground should be darker. Lighten the tones of forms as they recede into pictorial space. Forms also become less detailed and more indistinct as they recede into the distance. This simulates the changes affected by the atmosphere (lots of air) on the tones and colors of things seen in the distance.

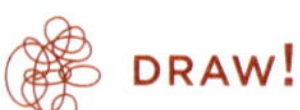

Create a surreal juxtaposition. For example, draw a concrete wall that turns into a waterfall, or a stall shower juxtaposed to a rainforest.

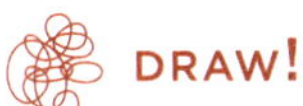

Please return to this page several times over the next few days to create layers of strokes. Across the entire surface of this page, make marks. The marks can be scribbled, hatched, brushstrokes, or handwriting. Cover the entire page.

Come back to this page on another day. Draw directly over the first round with any kind of marks you want. Come back another day and do the same. Finally, turn it into a seascape or landscape.

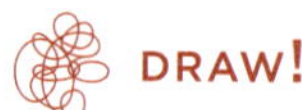

"Draw a garden gate."

—Dr. Nancy Lampert, Department of Art Education, Virginia Commonwealth University

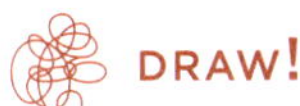

"Visualize a map of buildings from your childhood neighborhood. Create geometric shapes of equivalent sizes representing buildings. Make some shapes darker or lighter representing the importance of buildings to you. Use color to differentiate houses, commercial businesses, churches, government buildings, etc. Draw a heavyweight line between your house and buildings of major significance to you, a medium line between those with some significance, and a light line or no line between those that were not significant or rarely visited by you."
—April D. Allen, Ph.D., Assistant Professor, Interior Design, Michigan State University

Rose Gonnella

{ILLUSTRATOR AND DESIGNER. EXECUTIVE DIRECTOR, ROBERT BUSCH SCHOOL OF DESIGN, KEAN UNIVERSITY}

"*En plein air* is from the French language and means 'in the open air.' The phrase refers to the activity of painting directly from nature in the environment. However, drawing in the open air is also a wonderful way to explore mark-making on paper or a screen. The natural environment offers a vast richness of shape and form in a myriad of compositions on which to focus your creative drawing efforts.

"Using a range of good-quality graphic pencils (from 9H - HB - 9B), a hand-held sharpener; one hundred percent, thick cotton drawing paper; and a sturdy clip-board, trek out into the environment—sit, stand, search, observe; then stop when you find a small tapestry of nature that appeals to you. Begin your drawing with a line—that would be the horizon. Sketching out from the horizon, use as many different types of marks—short hatches, tiny dots, bold strokes, rough scratches, and/or long sinuous lines—that you feel interpret the shapes in your vision.

"Capture a single composition but allow the edges to be unrefined so the marks you make remain visible. The character of your pencil marks is what becomes the subject of intellectual interest beyond the natural forms. Drawing is the actual subject of your endeavor."

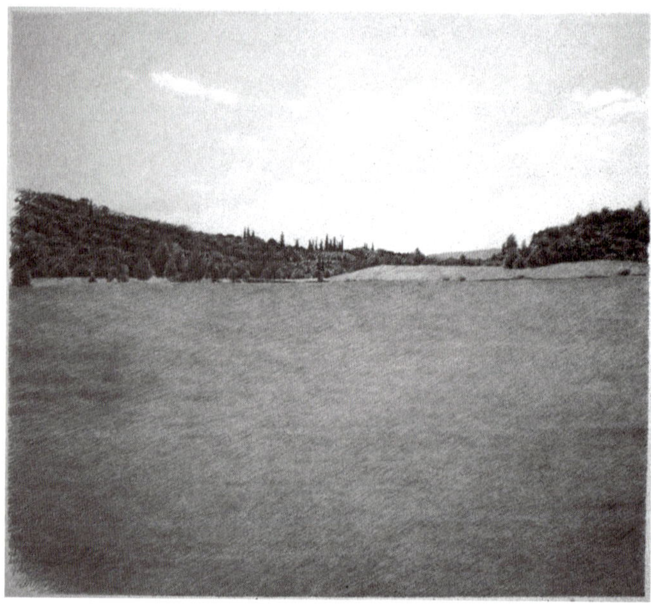

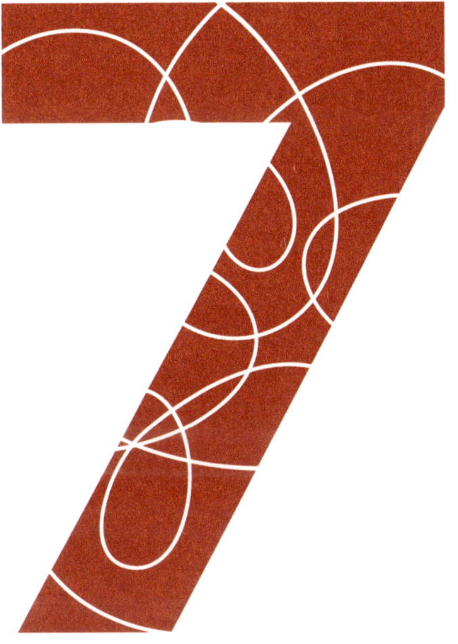

The Human Figure and Face

Looking at human figures and faces fascinates people. Studies show that even newborns show a preference for looking at faces. Artists and their patrons have favored the human figure throughout the history of art. Images of the human figure and face play key roles in cartoons, graphic novels, and general illustration, as well as in fashion design, graphic design, and advertising.

How do you convey a human gesture? How do you anchor a figure in pictorial space? How do you capture someone's likeness? How do you get a human figure scaled down to fit on a drawing pad? To accomplish any of these tasks, all of the drawing basics come into play, as does developing keen observational skills.

Convince your friends and family to pose for you. The more you practice, the easier it will be for you to quickly determine which aspects or edges of a figure you need portray to convey the figure's form or gesture.

Drawing the human figure and face is very challenging but keep drawing!

The Human Figure

Whether you draw a figure from life or from your imagination, understanding basic proportions helps tremendously. If you were to divide an average (not a very short or very tall person) human figure into horizontal slabs that are equivalent to the height of a human head, the breakdown would be:

1 = the head

3 heads = the torso

4 heads = the legs and feet

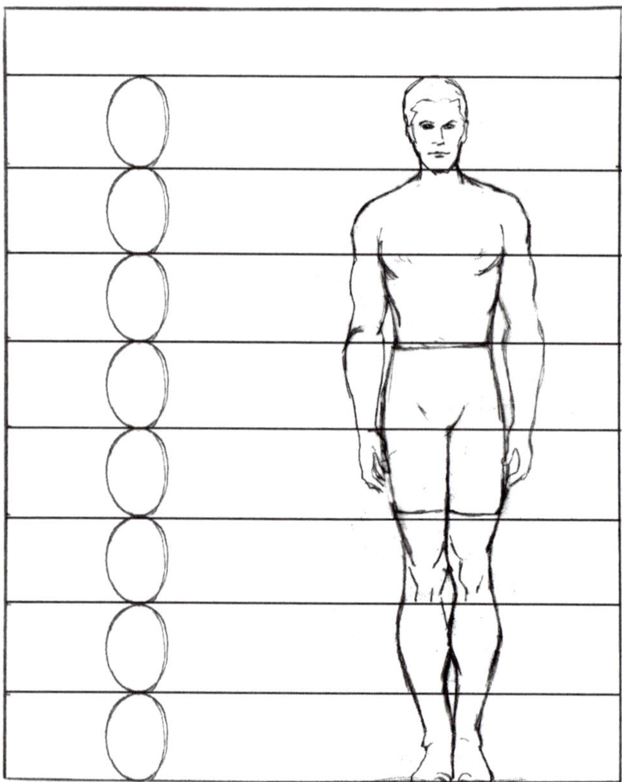

The average figure is about eight heads tall. Generally:

- Shoulders are wider than the hips.
- Elbows fall near the waistline.
- A hand falls about mid-thigh on a standing figure.

When drawing based on observation, always draw the proportions you see. Every person is shaped and proportioned differently, and depending upon the individual, the pose, and your point of view, these average proportions may need to be adjusted.

Rather than relying on your notions of what a figure or face looks like, you should keenly observe your subject matter.

Focus on:

- Visual reckoning—judging distances between and among forms
- Observing the negative spaces between a figure and the background or surrounding objects
- Determining the relative sizes of one part of the figure to another part and to the whole
- Scaling down what you observe to translate it to the size of the drawing paper
- Visually thinking about where the figure is in relation to the floor line, surrounding space and floor plane
- Specifically describing the contours and edges you see
- Determining which parts or positions convey the gesture or form of the figure
- Thinking of the lines you draw as the boundaries between the figure and the ground
- Assessing the distances between the features of a face

The Human Face

All of us find the human face fascinating, whether we look upon someone else's or our own, but challenging to draw.

What makes one person look different than another? The answer has to do with the size and shape of the facial features; the proportions of the features to the size of the face; and the distance between each feature in all directions. (As a reminder, proportions are the comparative size of one part to another and to the whole.) Try to draw based on what you observe, and practice a good deal. You might turn to self-portraits for the sake of an accessible (friendly) subject as well as for the investigative journey.

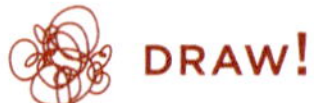

Ask a male friend to pose for you or use this drawn model. Use basic shapes (ovals, rectangles, triangles, etc.) to practice sketching the proportions of a male figure.

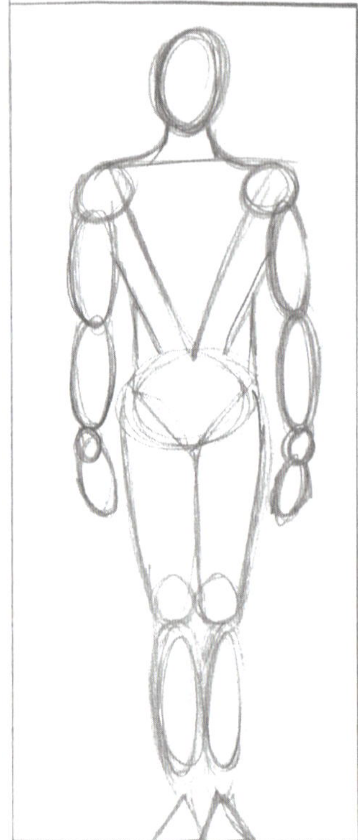

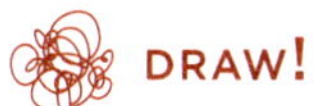

Flesh out the male figure shown below. Add details of your choosing.

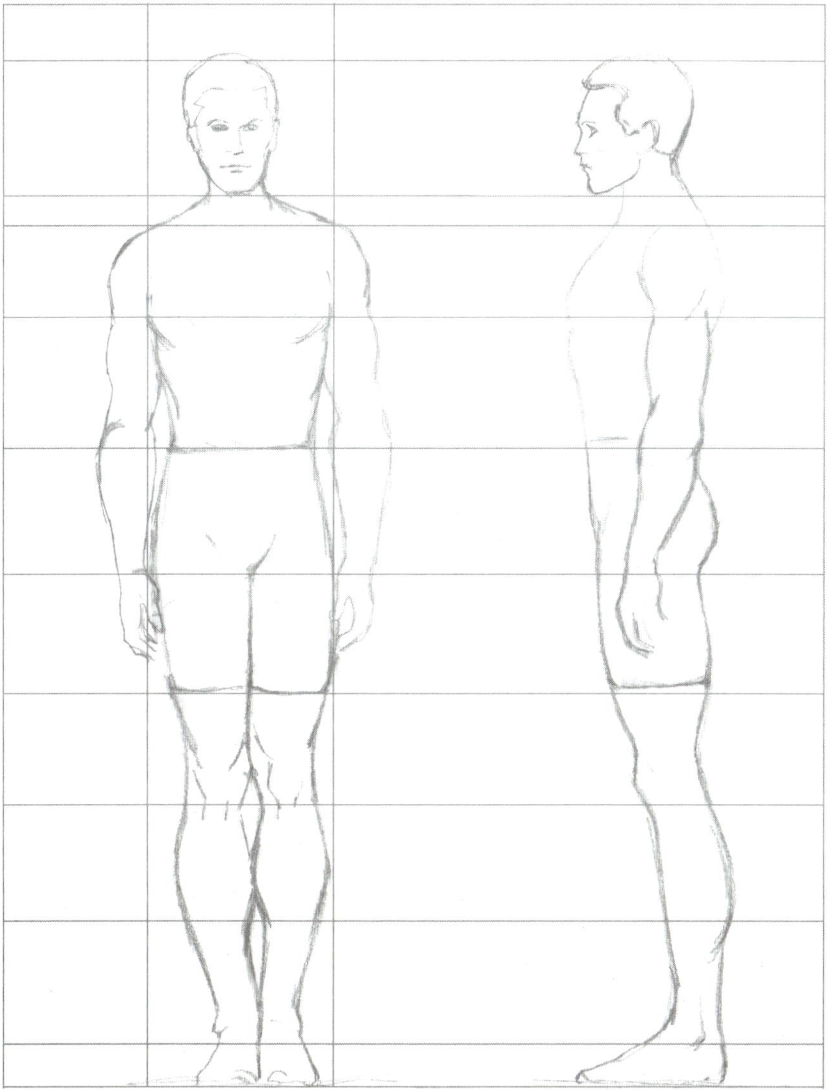

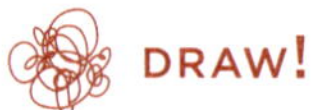

Ask a female friend to pose for you or use this drawn model. Use basic shapes to practice sketching the proportions of a female figure.

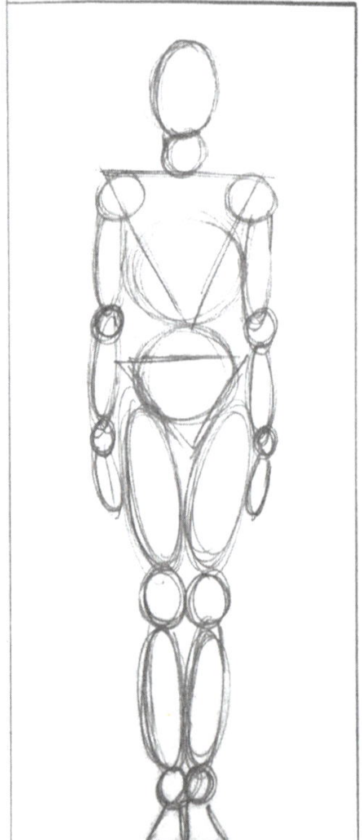

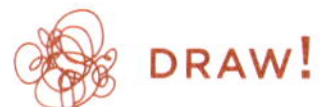

DRAW!

Flesh out the female figure shown below. Add some of your choosing.

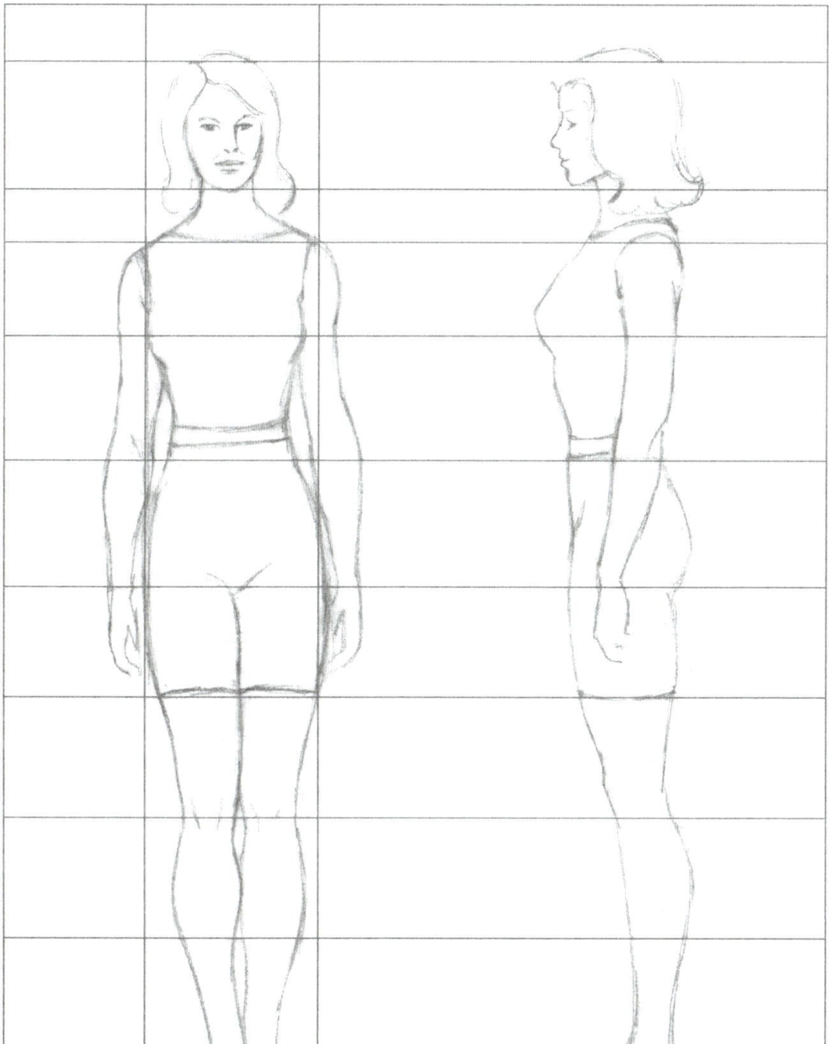

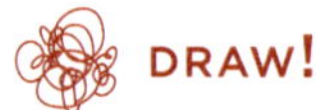

When a standing human figure is at ease—with the weight on one straight leg and the other leg bent at the knee—that is called a *contrapposto* stance. Due to the weight shift, the hips and shoulders tilt.

Ask a friend to pose for you in a *contrapposto* stance. Sketch your friend. To gauge angles, hold up your pencil to mimic the angle of his or her hips and shoulders. (Close one eye to line up your pencil with the the angles of the hips and shoulders.)

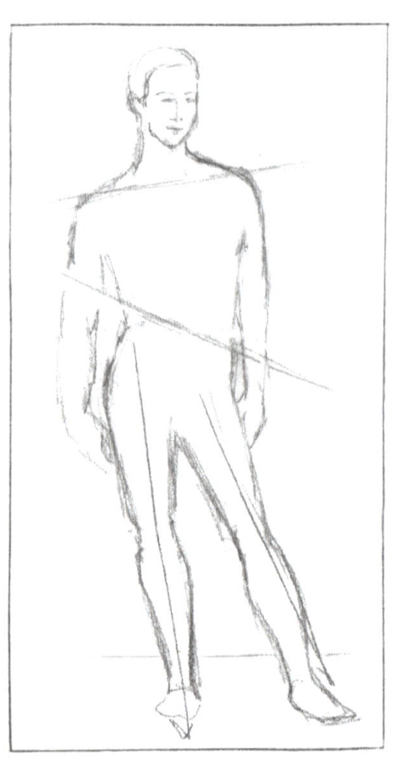

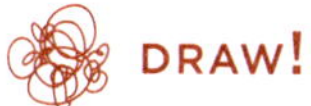

Visualize a human figure using simplified cubic shapes. (Sixteenth-century Italian artist Luca Cambiaso visualized human figures with simplified cubic shapes.)

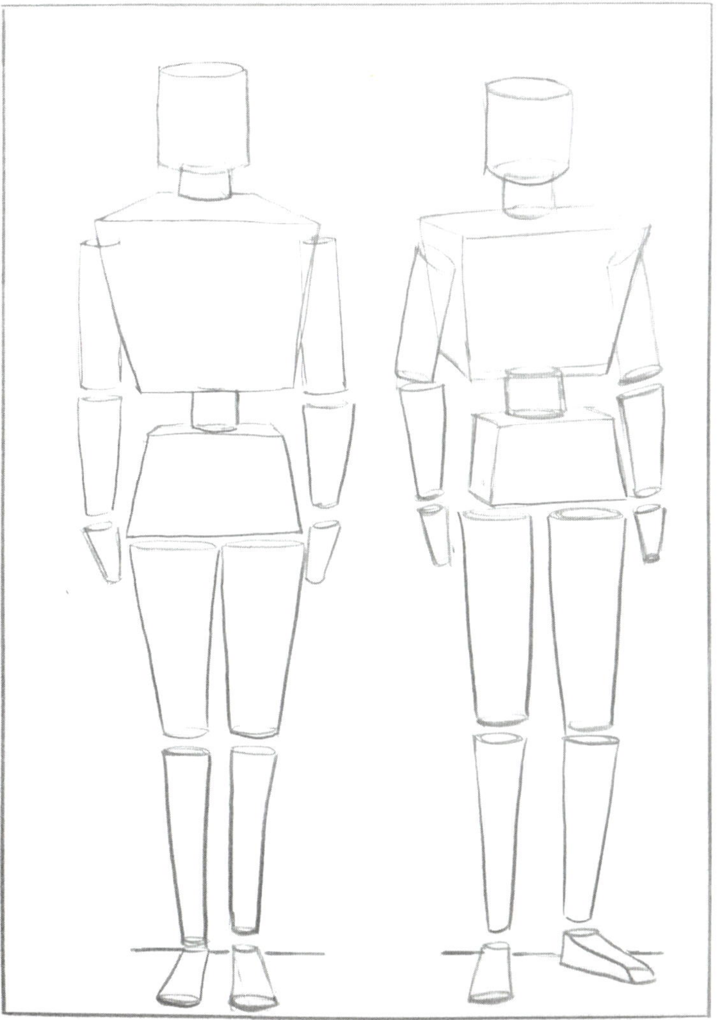

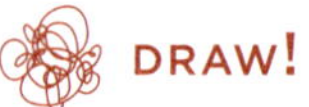

Ask someone to pose for you. Sketch him or her rapidly using fluid, sweeping lines to capture each body gesture.

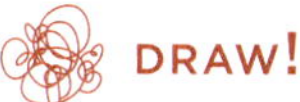

DRAW!

Ask someone to pose for you. Sketch him or her rapidly using swirling lines or scribbles to capture each body gesture.

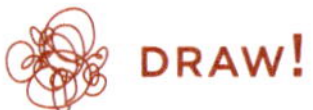

"Pick a word at random from the dictionary, then design a superhero from it!"
—Janna Brower, Artist

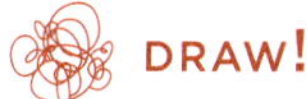

Ask a friend to pose for you with her hand on her hip. Draw the spaces between the arm and hip as well as all the other negative spaces you see. Refrain from drawing the figure itself.

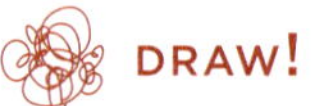

Draw a simple room space. Draw one figure in the foreground, one in the middle ground, and one in the background.

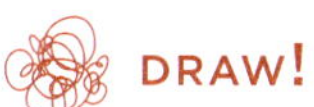

On the left-hand side of the page, draw a figure that is so big it is cropped—you see only part of it. Draw a full figure in the background.

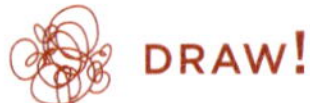

Sketch a huge, majestic figure in the center of the page. (Search online to see icon images of saints in Byzantine art or the genre of formal portraiture during the late Ming dynasty in China.) Embellish the background with patterns or however you like.

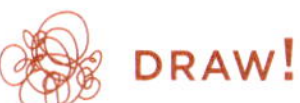

To learn to draw figures in movement, start with stick figures. Sketch stick figures running, throwing, swinging a bat, bending, lying down, and sitting.

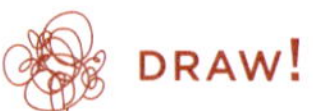

Sketch five figures performing an activity, for example, performing on a stage, hiking, or dancing (if you like, look up French painter Henri Matisse's *Dancers*).

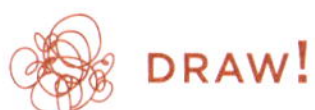

Ask a friend to pose. Draw your friend. After your friend leaves, draw your friend from memory. (Drawing from direct observation is a very different experience than drawing from memory or from your imagination.)

Storytelling: In this exercise, you are going to tell a story by drawing multiple figures.

Materials: Drawing paper, pencil and eraser, or marker; or digital pen and drawing tablet.

Subject matter: Choose a personal story or one from mythology, history, or literature—for example, the Chinese Fire Driller myth or the Battle of Marathon (490 B.C.).

1. Draw five major lines in relation to the edges of the page. Decide whether the lines will oppose the edges or parallel the edges. Movements that oppose (diagonals or curves) the edges of the page will appear more active or aggressive than movements that repeat the horizontal and vertical edges of the pages. These five lines will form the basic structure of your composition.
2. Develop (at least) two of these lines into figures, and turn the others into props, architecture, or environmental surroundings.
3. Go back and stress the original five major lines. Optional: On separate pages, draw individual studies of each figure.
4. Decide whether you prefer to use a linear style (a predominance of line to describe forms) or light and shadow to describe forms. Your narrative could dictate which drawing style you choose; for example, light and shadow might be better for more dramatic stories.
5. Any architectural or environmental elements should act as compositional supports for the action of the story.

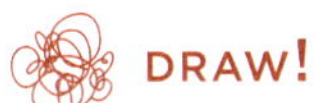

DRAW!

Using a fast (and loose) notation method of recording forms, sketch a contentious scene between two antagonists, perhaps one of them being yourself. The strokes and marks of this quickly made sketch —called a *pochade*—should communicate the emotional tone of the scene. The marks can be short, long, dark, light, stubby—any kind of mark except for deliberated.

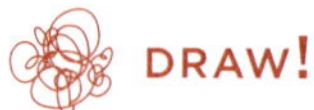

The trick to learning how to draw a face is to visually measure the distances between features. There are guidelines that can help you find those measurements. Draw a face utilizing the guidelines you see here.

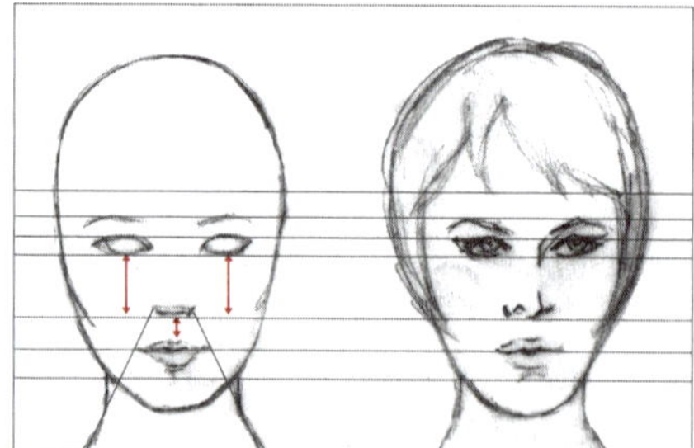

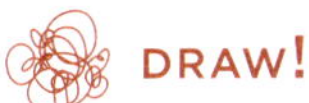

DRAW!

Close one eye. Look in a mirror. Use the technique of *sighting* to measure. Hold up your pencil to measure the distances between features—for example, the distance between the inner points of eyebrows, the width of the bridge of your nose, the distance between the bottom of your nose and top of your mouth, the distance between the outer corner of your eye and your face. Record the distances. Once you're done measuring, begin drawing and fleshing out the features of your face.

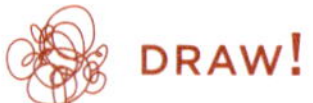

Look into a mirror. Draw dots on the page to represent the positions of the following: inner corners of your eyes; ends and arch of your eyebrows; your nostrils and your nose midline; the center of your closed mouth; and the end of your chin. Use those dots as the framework for a self-portrait.

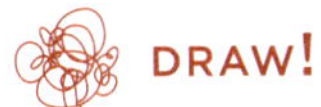

DRAW!

1. Look into a mirror. Draw a rectangle to denote the full area of your face.
2. Divide the rectangle into even vertical strips, approximately 1-inch wide. These strips act as zones for determining positions.
3. Inscribe the shape of your face in the rectangle.
4. Draw horizontal lines to denote the position of your eyes, the bottom of your nose, the middle horizontal of your mouth, the end of your bottom lip, and the end of your chin.
5. Use these guides to sketch a self-portrait.

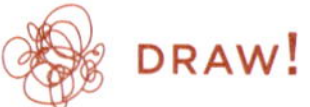

DRAW!

Illuminate a friend's face or your face from one side. Don't use overhead lights; instead, you should draw in a somewhat darkened room with the lamplight as the single light source.

Use vine charcoal or Conté crayon. Squint at your subject. Do you see areas of dark shadow? Sketch only those areas. Avoid details. Look for broad dark areas.

Look at the side of the face that is lighted. Draw a broad dark area behind the face to represent the background. That broad dark area will serve as the edge of the face. Behind the shadowed part of the face, the background should be a light value.

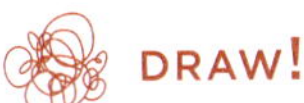

DRAW!

Using a continuous line technique, sketch someone's face. Without lifting the drawing tool point from the page, draw with an unbroken line. Draw continuously until you're done. A fine point marker works well for this.

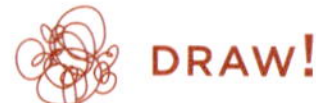

Cut-paper silhouette portraits date back to the sixteenth century. They were very popular in France during the reign of Louis XV and are named for his finance minister, Étienne de Silhouette, who enjoyed creating cut-paper shadow portraits. Contemporary American artist Kara Walker uses this medium.

Find black paper, precolored paper, or newspaper. Cut a paper profile of a friend. Some artists draw on the paper before cutting. Adhere it here.

Mary Ann Smith

{ARTIST, WWW.MARYANNSMITHWORK.COM}

Mood Sketch: "Draw yourself without looking in the mirror and express your state of mind."

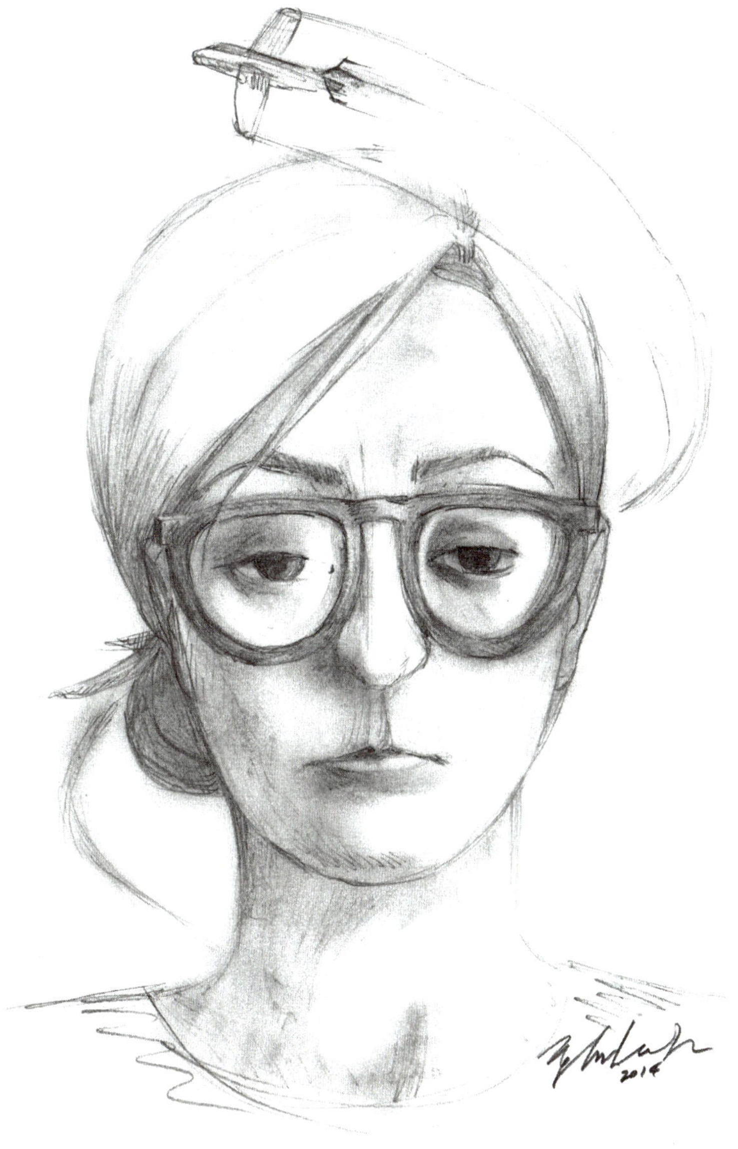

Lyman Dally

{ARTIST/ILLUSTRATOR, WWW.LYMANDALLY.COM AND HTTP://MUSCLEART360.TUMBLR.COM/}

"*Shape-sketching from photo:* Tear-out a photo page from a magazine, or find an 8x10-inch photograph that has good shadow/contrast in it. Place a piece of 9x12-inch tracing paper over the photo and tape it down over the photo. Using the side of a black colored-pencil point, sketch in the darkest shadow forms as they appear through the tracing paper. The tracing paper will act as a kind of filter, allowing darker shapes to be visible while obscuring finer detail. The idea is to create a convincing picture with only dark forms and very little edging line."

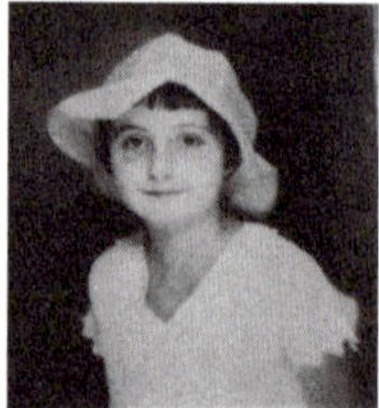

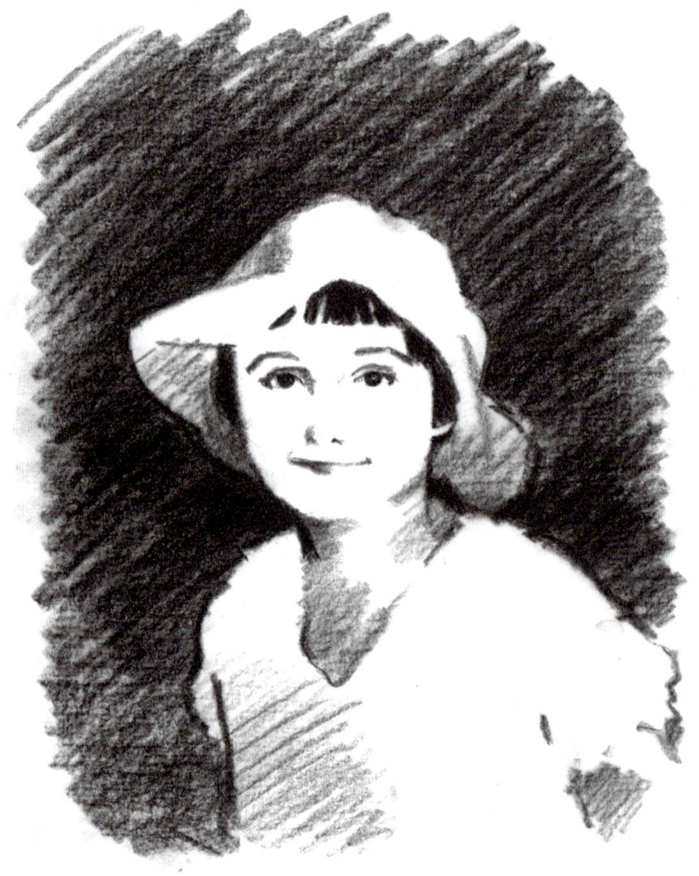

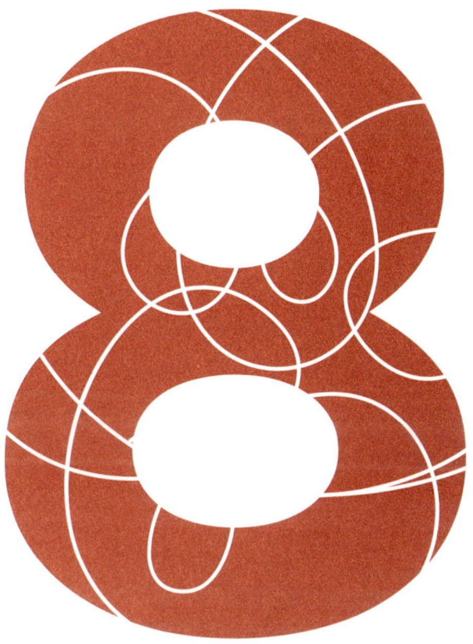

Experimentation

Contemporary artists, illustrators, and designers bend, stretch, and at times reinvent the drawing medium. There are rules and conventions from every era and culture, but people continually challenge them, finding countless ways to communicate expressively by making marks on a surface.

How you use the drawing medium is up to you. One way to go is simply drawing from observation. But there are many other ways. You can create accidental images or utilize symbolism. You can build the illusion of space, warp the picture plane, or combine graphic elements with letterforms. *You can experiment*.

The rest of this chapter is dedicated to expanding your drawing experience. Try each prompt, even if one seems too challenging or involves a process that you don't prefer. Some of the prompts relate to important art movements and key artists.

Multidisciplinary artist Greg Leshé points out, "Drawing is the most natural medium for channeling an 'immediacy' and connection between creative thinking and generating visual form(s)—the magic and immediacy of translating creative thoughts into tangible, visible forms for all to connect with. It's the basis of visual literacy and begins in our formative development in life. With practice, drawing becomes a powerful and essential tool for all practicing artists, designers, and visual thinkers."

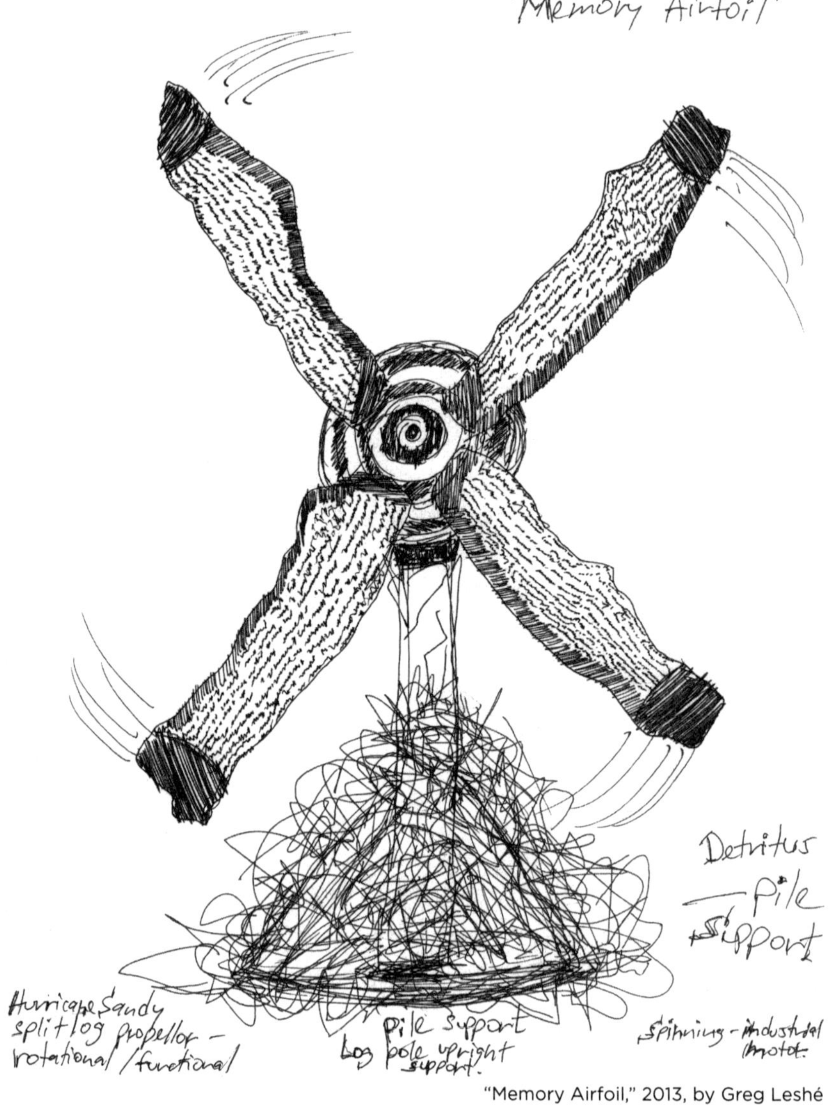

"Memory Airfoil," 2013, by Greg Leshé

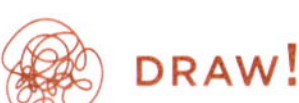

Draw abstractly. Rearrange or alter the representation of a figure or of a natural or manmade form to make it more expressive. (Visit the Metropolitan Museum online to see Pablo Picasso's *Man with a Hat and a Violin*, 1912.)

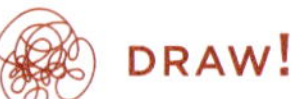

Express an idea or emotion using only shapes and colors, drawing from your mind rather than looking at anything. The drawing should be non-objective, significant in and unto itself, not depend upon anything else (symbolic or representational) for meaning. (Study the mature work of Russian artist Vasily Kandinsky who invented the term "nonobjective" to describe works with with no direct reference to objects seen in nature.)

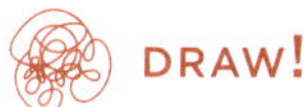

DRAW!

Cubist artists Georges Braque and Pablo Picasso represented their subjects from several angles at once and broke the forms of the subject into geometric planes (which critics called "little cubes"), challenging people's notions of visual language. For this drawing, think like a Cubist.

Depict an object or figure in an environment so that the distinctions between the solid mass and the environmental space are indistinct. Create contours and planed surfaces to define both solid form and void as well as to refer back to the two-dimensionality of the page.

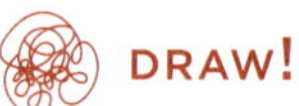

Use unconventional drawing tools, materials, and methods (for instance, draw with a squeeze bottle filled with food coloring or homemade ink, a paint-dipped Wiffle ball, or coffee cup rings) to create a drawing that challenges conventions or your own notions about visual art.

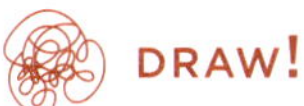

Draw an everyday scene or still life but add an element of incongruity or surprise. (Visit moma.org to see French painter Odilon Redon's *The Egg* or look at the work of Belgian painter René Magritte.)

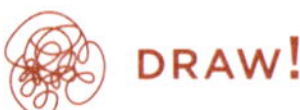

Create a drawing by chance. Tear up pieces of paper. Drop them on this page, then adhere them to the page just as they fell. Draw around, over, and next to them. Draw automatically; don't think about it too much. (Look up Automatism to discover more.)

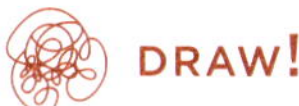

DRAW!

Apply ink or paint to a piece of paper. Then press that paper against this page, transferring an accidental image that results in a fractal pattern. Draw to elaborate on the chance visual. (And learn more about Decalcomania.)

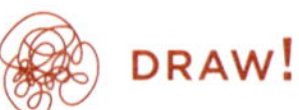

Using black acrylic paint or India ink, paint a huge biomorphic shape. Next, using a *grattage* technique (scratching or scraping a painted or inked surface with pointed tools), scrape the inked or painted surface with a key, fork, or both to create tactile appeal.

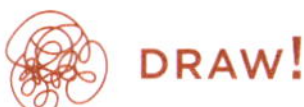

Draw with charcoal to create the illusion of spheric volumes that have a variety of textures on their surfaces. (Visit moma.org to see *Birth of Fly* by Polish artist Magdalena Abakanowicz.)

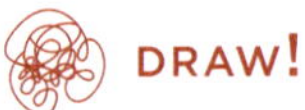

Use ink to make tangled lines that seem to form a long core of a dense web of knots. (Visit moma.org to see American [born Hong Kong] artist Paul Chan's *My baby's been through it all* and *Nasty Nets*.)

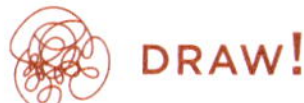

"Draw a dream—start with an element or scene that you remember, then map out the space in the dream. Tell the story of the dream with a sequence of drawings."
—Ruth Lingford, Senior Lecturer in Animation, Department of Visual and Environmental Studies, Harvard University

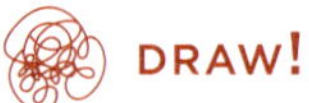

"Locate that point where an idea begins to form, then trace the path it follows through your mind until it is ready to use or share, and reveal a portrait of your process that someone else can understand."

—Dr. Glenn Griffin, Associate Professor of Advertising, The University of Alabama and coauthor of *The Creative Process Illustrated: How Advertising's Big Ideas Are Born*

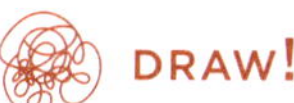

Incoporate disparate images from different sources to produce a personal history, perhaps a dreamlike scene. Create a pictorial interpretation of inner thoughts. Free associate. (Look up the work of Japanese artist Ryoko Aoki or visit moma.org to see her work.)

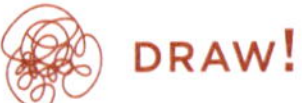

"Open a dictionary and, with your eyes closed, point to three different words on three separate pages. Using these words as a starting point, construct a pictorial narrative."
—Robert Brinkerhoff, Department Head and Professor of Illustration, Rhode Island School of Design

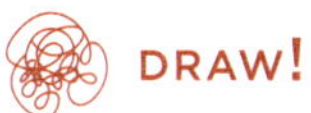

Find an object or detritus from your environment, such as a catalog, comic book, or discarded package. Use collage elements from the found object(s), then add your own imagery or marks to create a mixed media drawing. The theme is up to you.

Jennifer Sterling

{DESIGNER, HTTP://JENNIFERSTERLINGDESIGN.COM}

"Using the smallest black ink pen, draw a word of your choosing (for example, Hope).

Don't draw the typographic word... draw what it symbolizes to you on that day (for example, a child...walk...spiritual/religious symbol...clouds).

For thirty days draw a new word.

Take a photo of the drawing each day. At the end of the month, bring them into Photoshop. Increase the brightness/contrast and also delete the noise.

Layer each with a 'multiply layer' (in either Photoshop or Illustrator). Use for the basis of a poster."

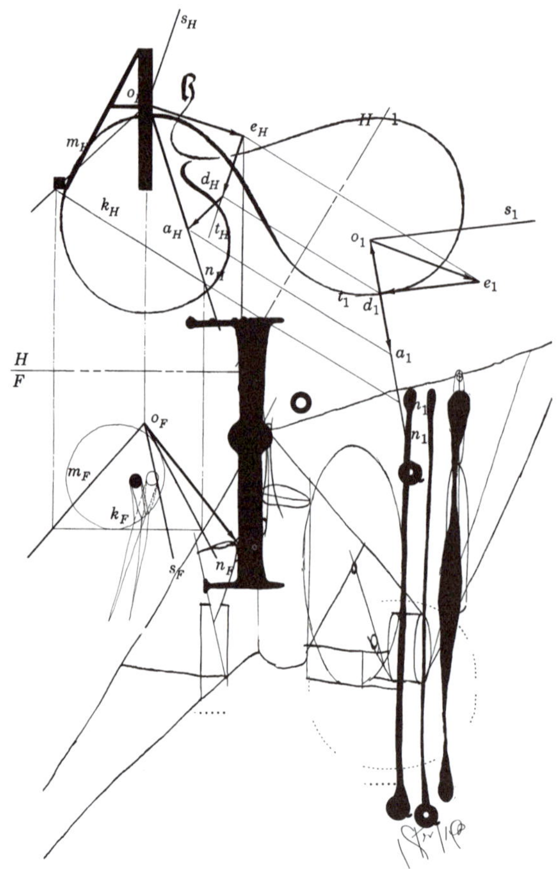

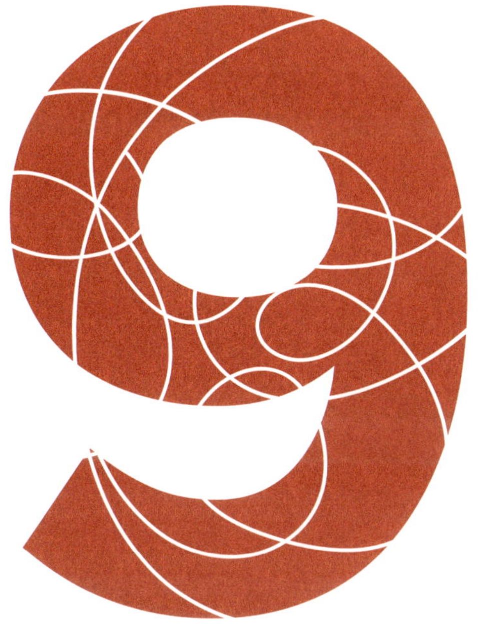

Creative Jolts

"I sometimes think there is nothing so delightful as drawing."
—Vincent van Gogh

At some point, every visual artist draws. Whether drawing is a daily practice, used to think visually, as preparatory sketches, or as one's chosen medium of expression, drawing allows you to explore, think, and feel. It may well be the most personal medium—it's easily autobiographical. It's also portable, and inexpensive, and seems like a natural extension of one's hand, eyes, and brain.

- Drawing is vernacular.
- Drawing is scientific.
- Drawing is industrial or commercial.
- Drawing is expressive.
- Drawing is conceptual.
- Drawing is ornamental.
- Drawing is fashion.
- Drawing is figurative.
- Drawing is visual thinking.
- Drawing is...

The prompts in this chapter will allow you to experience the expansiveness of what drawing is.

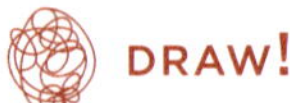

"We often forget the power that the image or symbol of a hand can have in drawing and design. Draw your hand, the one that is not holding the pencil or pen, in three poses:

- Cupping the bloom of a flower with utmost care and love.
- Giving the bloom as a symbol of hope.
- Crushing the bloom in anger and fear."

—Allan Drummond, Illustrator/Author

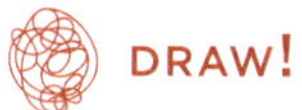

"Using an inkpad, transfer your thumbprint to the upper portion of the page. That is a head. Now add a body."
—Frank Viva, Viva & Co.

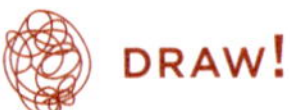

"On one piece of paper, make a drawing while looking at something in the world—a still life; make some more lines on that piece of paper while looking at a photograph, and then make some lines generated by your imagination."
—Jessica Stockholder, Artist/Professor, Chair of DoVA, University of Chicago

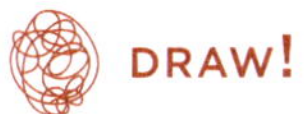

"Learn to be patient and thoughtful. Forget about aesthetics. Select a small problem to solve in the environment around you, something that you think, if more elegantly contrived, would save you time in your life and enhance your connection to the built landscape. Don't draw yet. Consider the same problem at the same time each day for one week. Obsess about it and reduce it to its very essence in your mind, then draw it. The beauty of your idea will emerge naturally from the elegance of your contemplative, reductive thought."

—Josh Owen, President, Josh Owen LLC, Associate Professor and Chair of Industrial Design, RIT

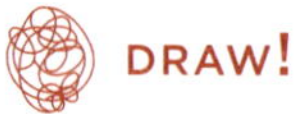

"Draw yourself as a box."
—Roberto Bertoia, Associate Professor, Art, Cornell University

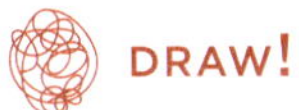

"Turn your trash can upside down and rescue the shards of things that seem meaningless: ticket stubs, gum wrappers, broken pencil tips, receipts. Make a collage that reconstitutes these elements so that they ignite some new narrative."

—Jessica Helfand, Senior Critic, Yale University School of Art

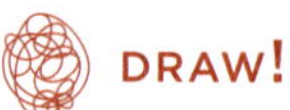

"Use charcoal to make a rubbing of a dimensional object on a sheet of paper. Cut the rubbing out and use it in a collage."
—Alexander Isley, Designer, Alexander Isley Inc.

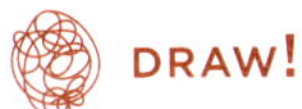

"Compile a list of nouns and adjectives that describe an object, space, or person. Be as specific as possible. Distribute the list to another person whose role is to visually explicate the textual description. Then have a third person compile a list of nouns and adjectives that describe this visual articulation, and pass that list to a fourth person. Continue ad infinitum."

—Laura Letinsky, Artist, Professor, University of Chicago

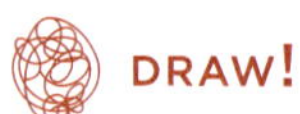

“Combine two animals to create a unique hybrid.”
—Shell Redfern, Program Manager, Design Studies, Southwest Florida College

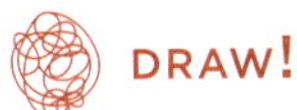

"Draw a place which you cannot enter but still can provide you with shelter and comfort."
—Kristina Junkroft, Architect

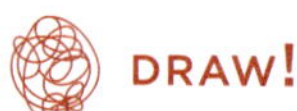

"Study a photograph of any moderately complex object. Now draw that object from a completely different angle."
—Michael Cho, Illustrator and Cartoonist

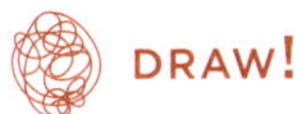

"Look at your hand. Picture it magnified 10,000 times—under the skin, through the fibers, and into the realm of molecules and atoms. Now picture the same hand from 1,000,000 miles above, from outer space, perhaps even beyond our galaxy. Draw the molecular realm along with what you see from deep space. Explore the similarities of micro and macro in our natural systems."
—Liz Blazer, Animator and Designer

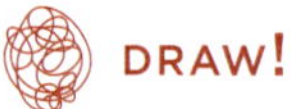

"Think back to yesterday and create a line drawing of the outfit you wore. Include as many details as you can remember."

—Kendra Lapolla, Assistant Professor of Fashion, The Fashion School at Kent State University

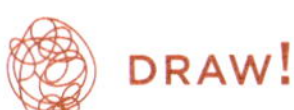

"Study a piece of wood. Look at the wood grains. Allow the pattern to play in your mind. See if the grain begins to suggest the shape of a face. Draw the face."
—Mark Romanoski, Artist

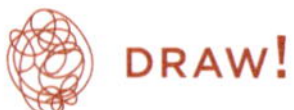

"Create a drawing that examines the past in order to better see the future. Draw an object demonstrating its development and progression over time (phone, tennis shoes)."

—Ted Rose, Professor, School of Music & the Arts, Cumberland University

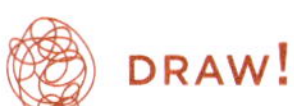

"Draw a happy ending."
—Jim Dawkins, Architect, Designer, Educator

Greg Leshé

{MULTIDISCIPLINARY ARTIST, WWW.GREGLESHEPROJECTS.COM, HTTP://WWW.GREGLESHE.COM/}

"Assemble a group of objects that you are connected to, that represent a personal history of experience, that are emotionally charged. Arrange the objects in a way that engenders a unique and unexpected narrative that evokes your psychic terrain. Draw that energy."

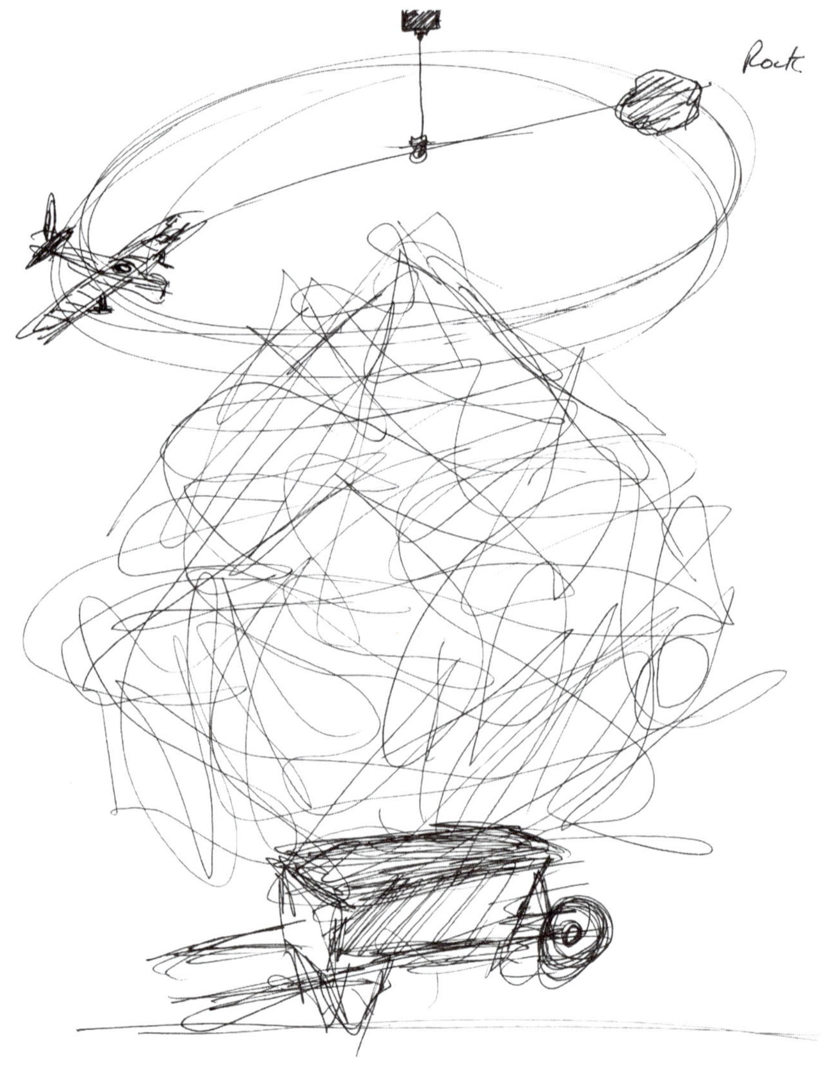

Denyse Mitterhofer

{DESIGNER/ILLUSTRATOR/ANIMATOR, WWW.MINENY.COM}

Give your paper some life! Draw a friend or a unique character. Deconstruct the figure into parts that can be attached with round-head fasteners. Cut out and fasten together. Now make it dance.

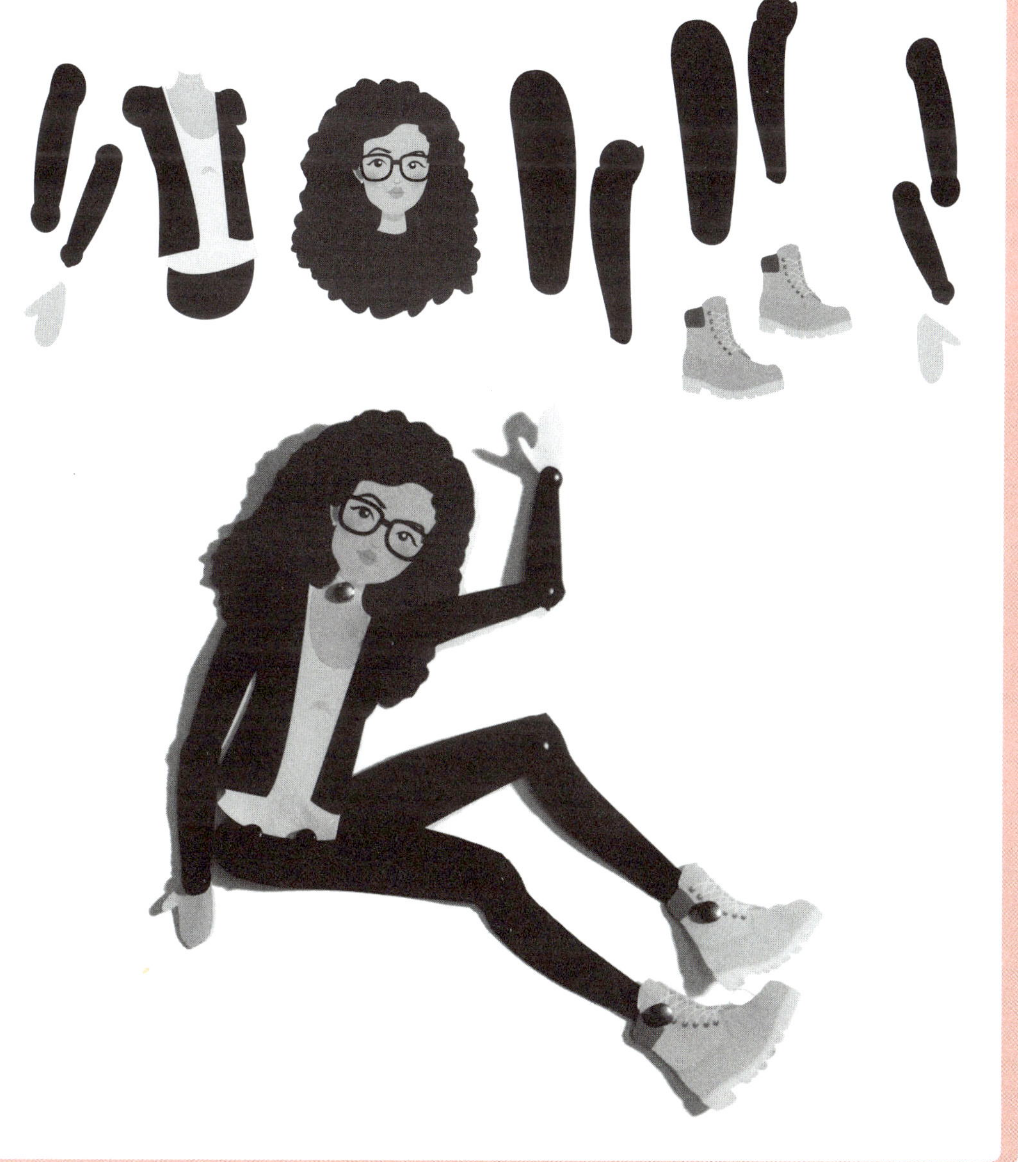

Glossary

abstraction: a simple or complex rearrangement, alteration, or distortion of the representation of natural appearance, used for stylistic distinction and/or communication purposes.

asymmetry: an equal distribution of visual weights achieved by balancing one element with the weight of a counterpointing element without mirroring elements on either side of a central axis.

background: what appears in the distance or lies behind the most important pictorial or graphic elements in the composition.

Baroque: a style of artistic expression prevalent especially in seventeenth-century Europe that is marked generally by use of complex forms, bold ornamentation, and the juxtaposition of contrasting elements often conveying a sense of drama, movement, and tension.

balance: stability created by an even distribution of visual weight among all the elements of a composition.

Chiaroscuro: an Italian art term referring to the visualization of contrasting light and dark tones employed to describe form in a drawing or painting.

cityscape: a view of a city or suburban environment as a subject for artists.

closed (or tectonic) composition: a composition where the marks or imagery appear held within the edges of the page. Often, elements parallel the edges. Internal drawn elements respond to the edges but all action stops at the edges.

composition: the form, the *whole spatial property and structure* resulting from the visualization and arrangement of drawn elements in relation to one another and to the page, meant to visually communicate or be expressive.

continuing line: lines are perceived as following the simplest path. If the line breaks, the viewer perceives the overall movement rather than the break; also called *implied line*.

counterform: the shapes defined within the letterforms, as well as the negative forms created *between* adjacent letterforms.

Cubism: visual art style of the twentieth century created by Pablo Picasso and Georges Braque, where artists reduce and fracture what they see and compose that scene, that figure, or those objects in a shallow space, often employing multiple vantage points.

emphasis: the arrangement of visual elements, stressing or giving importance to some visual elements.

equivocal space: ambiguous graphic spatial relationships, when interchangeable shapes (such as a checkerboard pattern) or an ambiguous figure/ground relationship is created, making the background and foreground difficult to distinguish.

eyeballing: drawing based on keen observation rather than on a system or schema, such as perspective.

figure/ground: a basic principle of visual perception that refers to the relationship of shapes, of figure to ground, on a two-dimensional surface; also called **positive and negative** space.

focal point: the part of a drawing that is most emphasized.

foreground: the part of a composition that appears nearest the viewer.

foreshortening: to shorten a form in the direction of depth to create the illusion of projection or extension in space.

fractured space: multiple viewpoints seen simultaneously, as in the Cubist style of fine art.

Golden section: a ratio used to structure compositions or shapes; as an equation it is $(a + b)/a = a/b$.

Grattage: a French term referring to a technique used to create tactile surfaces by scratching or scraping a painted or inked surface with pointed tools.

ground: shapes or areas created between and among figures; also called *negative space*.

high contrast: a wide range of values.

horizon line: a horizontal line in a composition that represents your eye level and the viewer's eye level; it usually indicates where land or water converges with the sky.

hue: the name of a color, for example, red, green, blue, or yellow.

iconography: symbols in works of art.

interstice: a space between forms.

illusion of spatial depth: the appearance of three-dimensional space on a two-dimensional surface.

illustration: a visual rendering that accompanies or complements printed, digital, or spoken text to clarify, enhance, illuminate, or demonstrate the message of the text.

light and shadow: light and dark tones employed to describe form; most closely simulates how we perceive forms in nature.

line: the path of a moving point—a mark made by a drawing tool as it is drawn across a surface.

linear: line as the predominant element used to unify a composition or to describe shapes or forms in a drawing.

low contrast: a narrow range of values.

middle ground: an intermediate position between the foreground and the background.

modeling with tone: the change from light to dark across a surface to create the illusion of volume.

module: any single fixed element within a bigger system or structure, for example, a unit on graph paper, a pixel in a digital image, a rectangular unit in a grid system, or a fixed encapsulated chunk of a composition.

naturalistic: an image created by full color or tone using light and shadow that attempts to replicate an object or subject as it is perceived in nature; also called *realistic* (although, in fine art, there is difference between the terms when referring to style).

nonobjective: a purely invented visual, not derived from anything visually perceived; it does not relate to any object in nature and does not literally represent a person, place, or thing; also called *nonrepresentational*.

open (or a-tectonic) composition: a composition that seems to go on forever, defying and somehow visually dissolving the edges of the page.

pattern: a rigid repetition of a motif methodically organized within a given field. The motif can be one or more shape or form—a dot, a line, a squiggle, a letterform, or a representational image such as a daisy or shirt.

perspective: a schematic way of translating three-dimensional space onto the two-dimensional surface. This is based on the idea that diagonals moving toward a point on the horizon, called the *vanishing point,* will imitate the recession of space into the distance and create the *illusion of spatial depth*.

picture plane: the blank, two-dimensional surface of a page.

plane: a two-dimensional surface bound by lines that defines the outside of a form; it has length and breadth, position, and direction, but no thickness.

Pochade: a French term for a quick sketch technique.

point: the smallest unit of a line and one that is usually recognized as being circular; also called a *dot*.

positive and negative: a basic principle of visual perception; refers to the relationship of shapes, of figure to ground, on a two-dimensional surface; also called **figure/ground**.

proportion: the comparative size relationship of parts to one another and to the whole.

repetition: occurs when one or a few visual elements are repeated a number times or with great or total consistency.

Renaissance: a humanistic revival of classical influence in Europe beginning in the fourteenth century in Italy, lasting into the seventeenth century.

rhythm: a pattern created by repeating or varying elements, with consideration to the space between them, and by establishing a sense of movement from one element to another.

saturation: the brightness or dullness of a color; also called *intensity* or *chroma*.

Rule of Thirds: a compositional technique using asymmetry to create visual interest and balance. The aim is to prevent the placement of the focal point at the center of a composition or to discourage placements that divide the composition in half.

shape: the general outline of something.

sighting: a visualizing technique used to determine the relative heights and widths as well as angles of the forms in one's subject matter.

silhouette: the articulated shape of an object or subject taking its specificity into account.

spatial relationships: the distance among the forms in a composition as well as between the things seen in relation to the viewer, how far/how close, and the shifts between near and far.

style: the quality that makes something distinctive.

stylized: emphatic unique treatment of form that moves away from a natural depiction.

symbol: an image having an arbitrary or conventional relationship between the signifier and the thing signified.

symmetry: a mirroring of alike elements on either side of a central axis resulting in an equal distribution of visual weights within a composition.

tactile (or actual) texture: a texture with real tactile quality that can be physically touched and felt.

texture: the tactile quality of a surface or the representation of such a surface quality.

transparent: see-through from one image to another, from one letterform to another, from one texture to another.

unity: when all the pictorial or graphic elements in a composition are so interrelated that they form a greater whole or are harmonious; all the pictorial or graphic elements look as though they belong together.

value: refers to the level of luminosity—lightness or darkness—of a color.

value contrast: the relationship of one element (whole, part or detail) to another, in respect to lightness and darkness.

variation: established by a break or modification in the pattern or by changing elements, such as the color, size, shape, spacing, position, and visual weight.

vanishing point: a point on the horizon line where diagonals converge.

viewfinder: an artist's tool—a clear plastic grid window for picturing compositions in thirds or other modular unit grids.

visual hierarchy: arranging pictorial or graphic elements according to emphasis.

visual texture: the illusion of texture or the impression of texture created with line, value, and/or color.

visual weight: the illusion of physical weight on a two-dimensional surface.

volume: the representation of mass on a two-dimensional surface.

Index

A

B

C

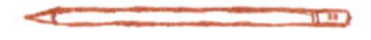

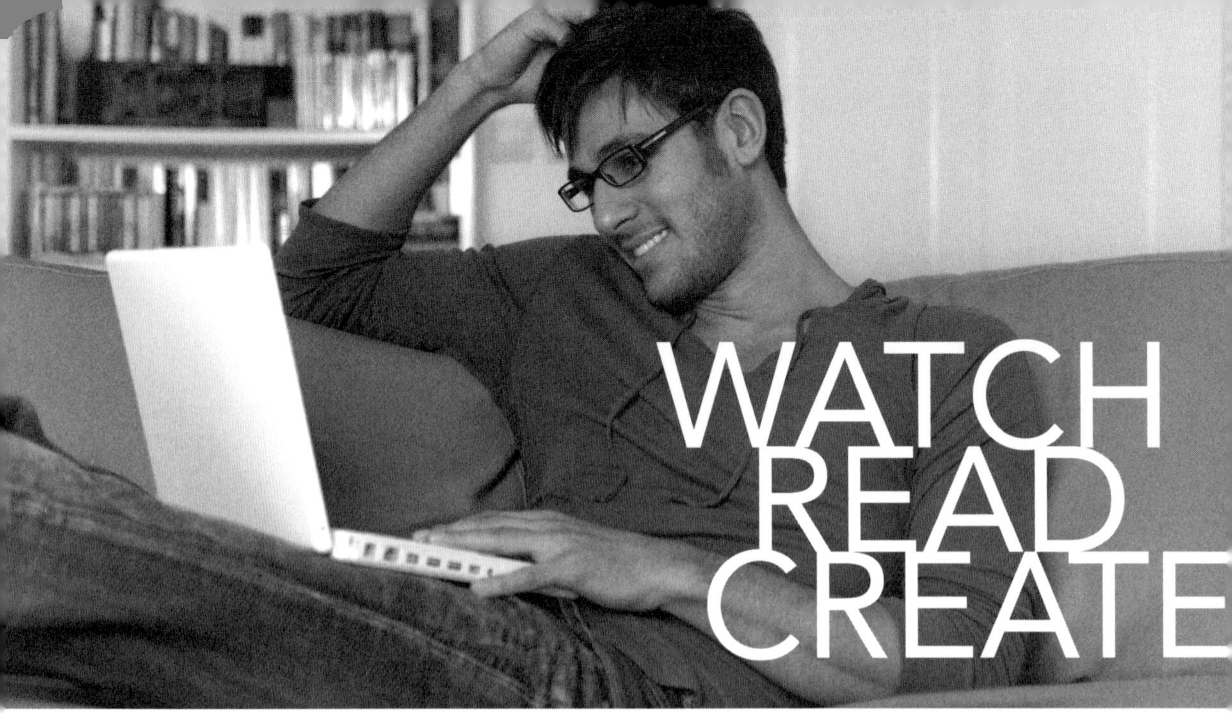